P9-BAW-831

THE
LIBERAL
UNIVERSITY

 J. DOUGLAS BROWN

Provost and Dean of the Faculty, Emeritus
Princeton University

THE
LIBERAL
UNIVERSITY

AN
INSTITUTIONAL
ANALYSIS

McGraw-Hill Book Company
New York   St. Louis   San Francisco
London   Sydney   Toronto   Mexico   Panama

The Liberal University: An
Institutional Analysis

PREFACE

In a field as broad as the organization and administration of universities, it should be a part of the contract between an author and the prospective reader that the author will present in advance the working specifications he seeks to follow.

It is the author's intention in this book to analyze the purposes, organization, policies, and processes of a particular type of university, that is, the "liberal university" as later defined. In this analysis, the aim has been to keep constantly in mind the interrelations, tensions and interactions normally present in the operation of an institution which must be responsive to many categories of constituents. The emphasis is, therefore, upon *how* these various elements and interests can be brought into moving equilibrium in advancing the mission of the institution. Ideas and values are the essential substance of the liberal university, but these must be nurtured within a viable, supporting institutional structure in which organization and policies encourage rather than restrict freedom and creativity.

With its emphasis upon the university as an integrated, operating organization, the book is more concerned with policies and administrative arrangements which can form a consistent whole than with a description of all possible variations in the parts. With the many surveys now available, it is often easier to learn about the more or less interchangeable bits and pieces of policy and organization in *many* universities than to see how such parts can be fitted together into *one* university. It is the hope of the author, after years in the practice and study of university administration, that both fellow administrators and friendly observers will find a study of the liberal university as an integrated "going concern" of value, especially at a time when tensions in most universities are unusually acute.

While this book is not a comparative, descriptive study of organization and policy in many institutions, its conclusions are based not alone upon intensive experience in a single institution, but also on years of rewarding interchange of ideas and experience with fellow administrators in other universities, including Harvard, Yale, Brown, Columbia, Cornell, Michigan, Chicago, Stanford, Wisconsin, and many other institutions in less degree. Such interchange has taken place in regularly arranged group meetings and on many campus visits. The author has also served for many years as a trustee of the University of Rochester and has been a consultant to other institutions. The reader will soon recognize, however, that the conclusions hammered out during twenty-one years as Dean of the Faculty and later Provost at Princeton form a central theme in the book. The author firmly believes that it is difficult to understand fully a complex human organization in all its subtleties unless one has lived with it for years.

It is also relevant to remind the reader that the author came to university administration after two decades of specialization in the study of industrial relations and organization. It has been a stimulating experience for a student of organization to move from theory to practice in a very complex type of organization. While one is in office there is, however, little time for introspective scholarship in institutional terms. But when one returns to an uninterrupted study of how human organizations function, the observations of two decades of deaning afford a rich accumulation of data which cries for analysis. The book is the product of that analysis, tempered by a far greater review of the experience and conclusions of others than the absence of footnotes would indicate.

While the judgments expressed in the book are the author's, he has been greatly helped by a critical review of parts of the study by his Princeton colleagues with special insights on various aspects of university activity. Among these have been Dr. Harold W. Dodds, President Emeritus; Dr. George P. Berry, Trustee; Dr. William S. Dix, Librarian; Prof. William J. Baumol; Prof. Fritz Machlup; Raymond J. Woodrow, Director of the Office of Research and Project Administration; Herbert S. Bailey, Director of the Princeton University Press; and Anthony J. Maruca, Executive Director of Administrative and Personnel Services. The author is especially indebted to his successor as Dean of the Faculty, Dr. Richard A. Lester, whose critical reading of the entire study led to many improvements in both content and presentation. Despite this generous help of his colleagues at Princeton and innumerable discussions with colleagues elsewhere, the author must take full responsibility for his conclusions on all phases of university policy.

J. Douglas Brown

CONTENTS

PART ONE

THE ELEMENTS OF A LIBERAL UNIVERSITY

PART TWO
ISSUES IN ACADEMIC POLICY

PART THREE
PROBLEMS OF ECONOMY AND CONTROL

PART FOUR

PROBLEMS OF EXTERNAL RELATIONS

INTRODUCTION

The Nature of a Liberal University

In the quaint language of our colonial forefathers, the liberal college was founded to produce "ornaments of the church and state." Early charters laid down the goals of "the advancement of knowledge and the education of young men." The content of the curriculum, the education of the faculty, and the future careers of the students all reinforced the concept that the function of the college was to improve the mind and sharpen the insights, moral and spiritual, of the students, rather than to transmit knowledge or techniques immediately useful in specialized occupations.

It can be argued that the colonial colleges were more "vocational" than their curriculum suggests. The usual college course, with its emphasis upon the classics, philosophy, theology, and disputation, did reflect the needs of the minister, lawyer, and statesman at a time when leadership of the young nation was in their hands. But to suggest that reading Greek and Latin texts or even vigorous debates on "The Meaning of Truth" was vocational in the modern sense is to stretch the concept severely.

Out of these beginnings grew a great tradition in American higher education which is still influential in our time. However, the opening of the West and the great expansion of agriculture, industry, and commerce, together with the shifting of interest from individual enlightenment of intellectual leaders to the improved competency of the thousands led, added a new focus in American education. While the older tradition persisted even in the newly established state-supported colleges and universities, a heavy overlayer of education as a preparation for specialized occupations by the transmission of specialized knowledge and techniques was superimposed. More important than the shift in content, however, was a subtle change in the focus of education from enhancing the general qualities and capacities of the mind *for its own sake* to improving the usefulness of the citizen in activities deemed by the state to be productive. This is, of course, an oversimplification, but the distinction, though usually the subject of much emotional debate, is real and significant.

Out of this evolution in higher education in America has developed a system of wholesome pluralism. Institutions vary in purpose, size, and support among themselves, and elements within institutions also demonstrate much diversity. Each of the many types of institutions has great contributions to make. It would be a severe loss if any one type should crowd out the others. It is to be hoped, rather, that the best elements of each type will become reflected in some degree in other types. Higher education in America is still in a fluid stage, and a strength of pluralism is the possibility of mutual reinforcement.

The subject of the following discussion is the university of the older tradition, arising out of the still older college. To differentiate this older type of institution, the expression "liberal" seems clearly appropriate. The *liberal* arts college in a number of significant instances has developed into the *liberal* university. Elements have been added in curriculum and scholarship, but the emphasis has remained sufficiently distinctive and effective in purpose and policy to justify the designation "liberal." The term is not bandied about by the institutions which uphold the tradition, because institutions are seldom introspective and because to be different is seldom considered a virtue in the American way of life.

Despite its deep roots in America's past, the liberal university faces troublesome forces of change in the years ahead. The welling up of vast millions of citizens into a prosperous way of life, the great expansion of productivity through science, technology, and effective industrial organization, and the great expansion of governmental resources and services all make the liberal university, which emphasizes age-old *individual* virtues and values, seem to some a bit of an anachronism. If so, it is an expensive anachronism. But the time has come to analyze what it is, or intends to be, and what its unique contributions are, before it is declared obsolete.

In the following summary of the attributes of a liberal university, the intention is to identify a type of institution for the purpose of discussing academic policies related to that type of institution. The image of an ideal liberal university has been put into sharp focus to emphasize its distinguishing characteristics. It has seemed preferable to postulate an ideal institution as the basis of discussion rather than particular existing institutions, since few observers would agree on the precise purposes or the precise degree of attainment of those purposes in any particular institution as complex as a university. With a defined prototype of an institution as the focus of discussion, the consideration of its policies, organization, and relationships can proceed with an emphasis on *principle* rather than on the diversity of *conditions* which any survey would bring forth. It is believed, however, that the principles considered have relevance in varying degree, at least, to a significant number of institutions.

1. The liberal university is man-centered and not knowledge-

centered. It assumes that knowledge is a means of education, not its end. The end is, first, the enhancement of the individual. His contribution to society is assumed to grow out of what he is as a whole person, primarily, and but secondarily out of what he knows or what techniques he has learned. It is this emphasis upon the individual that influences the whole system of instruction in a liberal university in terms of purpose, method, and such costly factors as a high ratio of teachers to those taught. There are real questions of optimum size of enrollments in *liberal* education, since it is difficult to keep the individual important in an environment of large numbers and complex organization.

2. The liberal university, reflecting the most fundamental needs of the individual, is *value-centered*. It does not assume that it can remain neutral and aloof from values, but rather that four or seven years of residence within its environment must have influence upon the value system of the student in a host of formal and informal ways. This does not imply indoctrination in any dogmatic sense, but the development of individual values through a complex of interactive processes—in the class, in the library or study, with the teacher alone, or with fellow students, preferably in a residential environment.

3. Emphasis of the liberal university is upon *fundamental* values and knowledge, not only because of tradition, but because such values and knowledge are those most challenging to the human mind and spirit. If knowledge is a means of education, it is assumed that great truths stretch the mind more than detailed facts.

4. To reflect its name, the liberal university seeks to assist in the *integration* of knowledge as well as its extension. This is more possible in an institution emphasizing fundamentals and in a faculty drawn together by the function of educating young persons in basic studies rather than one divided into specialized, vocation-oriented compartments.

5. The foregoing characteristics of a liberal university have led to an emphasis upon *independent study* and *individualized instruction*, to the extent feasible. Knowledge can be transmitted with some effectiveness in large lectures and classes. The hammer-

ing out of values and fundamental truths seems to require individual interaction between the teacher and the student, and between the student and a problem of special concern to him.

6. Withal, the liberal university justifies its special designation by emphasizing freedom—freedom of the individual to pursue self-education in things important to himself and not solely in preparation for the precise demands of a predetermined occupation. Such a university also, on its part, seeks to free men from ignorance, superstition, prejudice, arrogance, hatred, tyranny, greed, insensitivity, and cynicism and to strengthen their respect for the freedom and dignity of other free individuals in their self-fulfillment in all things good and beautiful. Further, such a university seeks to remain free from the restraints of well-meaning sponsors, whether in legislatures, churches, professional societies, or local communities. Individual and institutional freedom is bought at a price and must be safeguarded by both established rule and intuitive sensitivity in its implementation. In sum, freedom is or should be the pervasive climate in a liberal university.

7. Perhaps the most subtle characteristic of the liberal university is its ability to develop among its students and graduates a tradition of *individual responsibility* for public service. The more costly methods of instruction in such a university have usually led to a restriction upon enrollment. This, in turn, has involved an increasing degree of selectivity. Where, as in private universities, the criteria of selection could include indications of leadership and responsibility, as well as school grades or scholastic aptitudes, it has become almost certain that the ethos of the campus, reinforced by alumni attitudes and accomplishments, would be weighted toward public service. Traditions of this kind become deep-seated over time and, involving assumptions, are more effective than preachments.

8. Resulting from many of the emphases and attributes already suggested, an overall characteristic of a liberal university seems to be its development over time of a distinct institutional personality. Traditions in respect to assumed functions and values become ingrained. The seeking of integrity in structure and mission makes diversity of attitude toward institutional goals a little

less likely. Students and alumni—and even faculty members educated elsewhere—are caught up in a subtle pull of conformity and regard, of loyalty to a personalized entity. This is a valuable resource of the ongoing institution if the pursuit of excellence is maintained with unceasing vigor. If such an attribute shades into smugness and the easy assumption of superior virtue, it can become the virus of decay.

It is the purpose of what follows to discuss the constituent elements, functioning, and problems of a liberal university as here postulated. It is assumed that such a university is of moderate size. It is fully realized that the far larger universities which have now taken over the major burden of mounting enrollments will have different problems of organization. This does not necessarily affect purpose, however. Since the discussion will emphasize approaches rather than the details of organization, except for illustration, the variations caused by size will not be covered. The reader is again reminded that, in order to bring out principles more clearly, a *type* of institution is postulated and not any particular existing institutions.

To some, the characteristics of a liberal university which have been outlined may be considered the ideals for a liberal *college* and much too concerned with the education of the whole man, rather than with training in a particular subject, to apply to the graduate levels of instruction in a university. The emphasis is, however, intentional to sharpen a distinction which must be made in the trends in higher education in the United States.

The university in the United States is of mixed heritage. The undergraduate college has its roots in the Anglo-Saxon tradition of educating young men for positions of leadership in their society. Our graduate schools—a much later development—have been a carry-over of the German emphasis upon advanced scholarship rather loosely superimposed upon the undergraduate college. We are still in the process of integrating these two traditions. In some institutions, the Anglo-Saxon tradition has continued to influence the whole program of the university. While tensions exist, it is this type of institution which can be called liberal. Undergraduate education has been raised in quality and intensity to move toward that of graduate education. Graduate education, especially in the arts and sciences, has absorbed *in some degree* the climate of education of the whole man. Graduate schools in such institutions have usually maintained close relations with their undergraduate college, through both a common faculty and the bridging of programs of instruction and scholarship in method and across disciplines.

In other institutions, because of increasing enrollments, the wide diversity of subjects taught and the emphasis upon subject matter, techniques, or the immediate qualification of students for useful employment, the shift to a professional or vocational orientation has become pronounced. This has occurred in undergraduate programs and even more at the graduate level. These institutions, no matter how worthwhile their contribution, have become what has been termed "multiversities." Usually publicly financed, they have reflected the current desires of their students and the public in a society where old traditions are less strong. They have found it difficult because of their size to preserve a concept of the integration and interrelationship of learning and, especially, to sustain a tradition of education of the whole man.

It would be useless to rate American universities on a scale from most to least "liberal" in the respects outlined. Universities are not internally homogeneous institutions. The distinction can not be drawn according to source of financing, although private universities have been freer to determine their character for themselves. Size is most certainly a factor, but not necessarily a bar to a liberal tradition in at least some segments of the institution. Selectivity on admissions and a high ratio of faculty to students are perhaps the most common attributes of institutions which emphasize the education of the whole man.

In the analysis which follows, the problems of the liberal university are the focus of discussion because they are different in considerable degree from those of the multiversity. It is the premise of the study that the survival of the liberal university in America is of great importance to the health of the nation, since its goals are the education of leadership and the preservation of our cultural heritage in its mutually reinforcing elements. The aim of the study is not so much to prove the value of the liberal university, since this must be a matter of faith. Rather it is to analyze the problems of the liberal university in a time when it is caught in powerful crosscurrents, both economic and educational, which will greatly influence its future.

PART ONE

THE
ELEMENTS
OF
A LIBERAL
UNIVERSITY

1

THE ORGANIZATION OF A LIBERAL UNIVERSITY

Despite its limited size in an era of bigness, a university is one of the most complex of human institutions. This fact arises partly from the diversity of approaches to knowledge and understanding and partly from the manifold interests and concerns of individuals who teach and learn in these diverse areas. It is also a concomitant of the condition of relative freedom of initiative and activity which must exist in scholarship and learning. A university, and especially the liberal university, is greatly dependent upon the response of its members to *general* obligations and assumptions and, in its academic operations, very little dependent upon command.

In this, the university is sharply different from industrial organizations. Even in its supporting services, the concept of mission is a key source of effective performance, since material compensation is at best but modest.

In order to sustain response to general obligations and assumptions in a liberal university, there must exist strong leadership, ready and effective communications, and a vital and consciously recognized sense of tradition. Leadership which operates through response must be more sensitive and more farsighted than that which operates through command. A large part of the function of such leadership relies upon the communication of ideas and of the reasons for policy and objectives, not upon the promulgation of directives. The passing on of traditional assumptions and expectations is one of the most subtle yet most necessary arts of university leadership.

Change in a liberal university may come slowly, not alone because of resistance to change itself, but because of the need to fit change within a vital framework of tested tradition. Only when consensus on the value of change is gained is the time ripe for action. For this reason the organization of a university involves many devices for review and concurrence which might frustrate the dynamic industrial executive. A clever decision on the part of the latter may sell more soap and soon be profitable in dollar terms. A decision affecting an educational process may require the cooperation of hundreds of faculty members and take years to prove its value.

Not only must the organization of a liberal university emphasize response to ideas emanating from central leadership, but it must provide sensitivity to pluralistic initiative and widely diverse points of judgment. The sources of ideas and the loci of judgments occur in every school, department, and program, as well as in a broad spectrum of functional and status categories: the general faculty, administrative officers, staff, student body, alumni, trustees, donors, and the government. Any university is a "public" institution in the sense that its policies and activities are of interest to a widespread clientele, internal and external. The judgment upon a prospective candidate for appointment or for course credit is a decentralized one in first instance. It must, however, be brought within a system of standards and procedures for which the university, as such, is responsible. Not only in respect to formal recommendations for appointments or degrees must the communication system of a university be highly effective, but also in assuring the ready flow of myriad ideas, criticisms, and queries that are the by-product of an institution which emphasizes freedom of expression and group consensus rather than command.

The diversity of parts and constituencies, no matter how demanding of the administrator's patience and understanding, is a source of great strength in the liberal university. Pluralistic initiative may result in marked variations in the growth and dynamism of different elements at different times. At one time a number of disciplines are forging ahead, because of either internal leadership or national interest. Many others are moving along satisfactorily. Some are marking time because leadership has faltered, attrition has been excessive, or the field has lost purpose or interest. The presence of vigorous departments helps faltering departments to sustain confidence while reconstruction proceeds. The general standing and confidence of the faculty as a whole help in the repair of the weaker parts. In the same way, a continuing support of one constituency, perhaps the younger alumni, helps offset the concern of older alumni that the institution has departed from sacred ways. Even in the criticism of new ventures in campus architecture, there will be at least two sides to the argument.

But pluralistic initiative and the diversity of constituencies within a liberal university become a source of danger unless the leadership of the university assumes positive responsibility in resolving ideas into policy. Leadership remains leadership and not merely the function of mediating different points of view or different interests. The university must be organized to expedite a decision when all parties have been heard. The university is not a debating society or a legislature, even though a university faculty sometimes encourages this impression. It must be repeated: a liberal university must exercise leadership, assure ready communication, and uphold vital traditions to survive and accomplish its function in society. It is not the passing reflection of any constituency, internal or external. It is something of itself. It must sustain its personality as a perpetual institution. Its organization must be designed and developed with this end in view.

In a time when the availability of funds, whether adequate or not, receives close attention in higher education, it is difficult to withstand the temptation to permit financial considerations to push aside academic considerations in the determination of institutional policy. Because of its traditional mission, this is a serious hazard for the liberal university. Given the wide variety of sources of funds today, nothing can be more undermining to the integrity of purpose of the liberal university than the easygoing sanction, "If you can get the money, go ahead!" The essential economy of all worthwhile endeavors must be appreciated, but the economic test of the mission of a liberal university lies in returns in talent, ideas, values, and knowledge in the long future and not in the availability of ready dollars for ready results in size of staff or facilities. The organization of a liberal university must provide checks and balances to assure economy in terms of its chosen mission and not in terms of its current balance sheet alone. This adds not only to the responsibility of leadership, but to the necessarily sensitive mechanisms of internal control of highly diverse enterprises.

The best answer to opportunistic response to outside offers of funds as a determinant of policy is the vigorous development of forward academic planning apart from the immediate availability of funds. This is probably the greatest single need in university operations today. Many universities have been hesitant to mix academic planning and business planning for fear of mutual contamination. But the time has come for "academic management" with a keen sense of both mission *and* economy, now *and* in the foreseeable future. This concept must find its place in university organization with all the delicate interrelations necessary to make it effective. A very old and valuable type of institution, the liberal university, is now moving into difficult times. It must prepare itself for the problems and opportunities which lie ahead.

The liberal university must become introspective about its internal organization even though a vital segment of its leadership, the faculty, has traditionally been suspicious of organization. To the faculty, organization suggests administrative arrangements which limit freedom and committee meetings which waste time. The improved organization of most universities will require both more effective and responsible administrative leadership and more effective and responsible faculty committees to participate in policy development. Faculty members must learn that poor organization is a far greater threat to their ability to teach and carry on scholarship in the way they want than responsible executive leadership in a carefully developed organizational structure. The administrative structure of a university provides the framework within which the essential operations of teaching and scholarship are carried on. It should be responsive to the needs and aspirations of the student, the teacher, and the scholar in the fulfillment of the total mission of the university. Under present-day conditions, an outdated and cumbersome organization or a weak and passive administration may undermine not only the effective use of academic freedom, but the survival of the institution which should provide it.

Against this background of the general characteristics of organization in a liberal university, it is useful to seek to analyze many specific problems, issues, and policies in relation to the diverse elements or constituencies which make up the institution. Unlike a watch, it is difficult to take a human organization apart and still see how it functions. Physiology, including study of the delicate interactions of nerves, hormones, and psychological stimuli, must supplement the simpler analysis of apparent anatomy. At best, the study of the university in action must be impressionistic, with heavy reliance on personal observation by the same observer. Cross-checks among institutions are valuable, but to learn fully the physiology of diverse institutions requires longer and more intensive involvement in them than most students are likely to experience. Despite the lack of objective proof in any study of human organization and relations, some worthwhile conclusions are possible which may be suggestive to those concerned with improving the effectiveness of a complex, evolving institution.

The elements or constituencies of the liberal universities which will be considered are: the presidency, the faculty, the administration, the trustees, the students, and the alumni. Since each element interacts with each other so continuously in the life of the university, it will, in each case, be considered a point of entry into the study of total organization rather than a neatly separable part.

2

THE
PRESIDENCY

As in all human organizations in which effective accomplishment of mission is dependent more upon response than upon command, the leadership of a liberal university must center in a presidency which assures by its visibility, status, and structural orientation that the influence of the president will pervade the institution. With its emphasis upon the individual, whether teacher or student, and upon the values and assumptions of all engaged in a common enterprise, the organizational focus of leadership in a liberal university must be in a person who himself, as an individual, represents in attitudes and policy a coherent system of values and assumptions. An industrial organization may seek to merge the functions of leadership into a combination of senior specialists in production, finance, and public relations, not always successfully. A church, in order to safeguard its traditions, may place leadership in a collective body. But the university not only deals in a host of intangibles rather than profit, but also must move forward with vigor and sensitivity. Therefore, only a person, a president, can effectively combine tradition and vigor to gain understanding response from a complex of cooperating constituencies.

It can be argued that the position of president in a *liberal* university should be stronger in organizational terms than that in a great service institution—a multiversity—with scores of schools and programs. In the latter type of institution, the president may become, in increasing degrees, a chief, coordinating administrator assuring the economic health of the university. The determination of goals, academic standards, and educational policy is more likely to be decentralized. This may be necessary as institutions become larger and the functions of the chairman of the board of trustees, the president, and the chief educational officers of the institution become more distinct. In such a situation, there may be a tendency for the president to become a mediator between the board, representing a broad, external constituency, and the educational leadership of the institution.

But the president of a liberal university must be himself the articulate spokesman, both internally and externally, for a tradition and for the appropriate interpretation of a tradition in the face of complex issues in which economic and educational aspects are closely intermeshed. He can ask the advice of his board and of his faculty, but there are times when he must assume final and lonely responsibility for judgments upon which group consensus is not easy to reach. Some of the more recent difficulties which have beset large and strong universities give one reason to believe that when the chips are down, the president should be the spokesman of the board, the faculty, and the institution as a whole. Neither students nor faculty nor the outside public will recognize a board chairman or a provost as the personal embodiment of the conscience and intent of the institution.

It is believed preferable, therefore, in a liberal university for the president to be the senior and chief officer of the board of trustees, as well as of his faculty and administration. In this way he brings to a focus within himself the various predilections of these as well as other constituencies. This is not always a happy position, but it is one made necessary by the character of an institution which deals in ideas and values and must resolve the diverse responses of freethinking individualists. Since the values of an individual must be resolved in a person, the values of an institution dealing in values must be resolved in a person. A president may sometimes err in his sense of the appropriate, but in matters requiring subtle interpretation of institutional tradition it is preferable to have a resolution of values in a single well-informed and responsible person rather than to rely upon the highest common factor of group judgment.

This does not imply that the president should be free to determine educational or financial policy without the concurrence of his faculty on the one hand or of the trustees on the other. Rather, he should be free to judge, after all considerations are discussed, what he believes to be the proper course of action for his institution. The wise president, whether the ideas or proposals for action are his own or those of others, will encourage free discussion and all appropriate consultation before forming a definite conclusion. But once that conclusion is reached, it is consistent with the nature of a liberal university that he take responsibility for the idea or proposal and exercise his influence to gain favorable response. The division of responsibilities within the university is such that he cannot passively permit the faculty to come to loggerheads with the trustees, or the administration with the faculty. As the chief judge and initiating element in all three constituencies, he should be ready to stand and be counted. In the well-run liberal university, this attitude of leadership is assumed and expected. It is in the faltering institution, with a cautious and passive president, that the delicate balance of constituencies deteriorates into factional pressures and counterpressures.

If the preceding analysis of the function of president in a liberal university suggests that the position is a difficult one to fill, this is the intention. The president of a liberal university can be assumed to have not only all the responsibilities of an industrial executive, but in addition functions of leadership and representation in terms of traditions, values, and ideas which an industrial executive sometimes timidly avoids or leaves to a specialist in public or industrial relations. But the liberal university is a "public" institution in terms of its influence upon young people, society, and the body politic. It cannot be led effectively by a good housekeeper, a good money raiser, or a good professor, if any of these ignores the central core of the role. A president must be far more than any such useful types of persons. A number of universities have found this out to their sorrow.

Apart from the central role of leadership in terms of the goals, values, and standards of his institution, the president must have a sense of organization and of the administrative arts of working through organization to attain institutional goals. It is this aspect of his role which makes a shift from professor to president most difficult for many. The professor can express ideas and purposes with fluency, but the president must implement them through the complex processes of gaining willing and effective action in scores of areas and at all levels. It is in the balanced interplay of leadership in ideas and leadership of an operating, dynamic organization that the quality of a president is tested. Too much emphasis on either aspect at the expense of the other may lead to high purposes without accomplishment or a well-run educational factory.

In summarizing the most critical aspects in a president's role as an administrator, a former president of long experience in the position who is also a lifelong student of administration has listed three areas as primary: "(1) The practice of consultation, (2) The principles of delegation, and (3) The structure and staffing of administrative organization." * The first, the practice of consultation, is peculiarly important in a university organization in which sensitivity to response is vital to accomplishment. The second, delegation, is at the core of the concept of organization as opposed to the solo arts of the professor. It involves the determination not

---

* Harold W. Dodds, *The Academic President—Educator or Caretaker*, McGraw-Hill, New York, 1962, p. 72.

only of the functions to be delegated, but of the people who can best perform them. It also requires a fine sense of degree of delegation, of what oversight is to be maintained, and of how and when the results of delegation are to be audited.

The third area, the structure and staffing of administrative organization, involves the constant task of a chief executive to fit functions and people together into an effective operation. There is some danger in an academic environment that organizational structures will be allowed to grow of themselves so long as the job gets done by someone. But unplanned or outdated structures can waste effort and cause friction even with the best of personnel. With good organizational structure, not only is the effectiveness of personnel enhanced in performing present tasks, but the capacity for institutional change and growth is enlarged. It is the wise president who not only chooses staff carefully but senses the best arrangement of functions and relationships which will utilize their capacities fully.

In the delegation of responsibilities, it is more likely that the president of a liberal university, with his heavy obligations to maintain leadership in the educational functions of his institution, will need to rely upon a strong supporting staff in the investment and control of funds. The investment of endowments has come to be a task for experts, whether through retained investment counselors or a full-time staff. The trend has been toward the use of outside specialists under the general guidance of a committee of the board of trustees and the close supervision of a financial vice-president. The latter, in turn, has become the internal expert in the development of modern accounting and budgetary operations. Although the final judgments in the use of funds are the president's, the investment and control of funds, as such, can be readily delegated.

The development of external sources of new funds involves a different combination of problems for the president than the conservation and control of existing funds. The decision to support a liberal university is so likely to be based upon the purpose and personality of the university that the president as the chief spokesman and symbol of purpose and personality must play an influential role. Even with the best of staffing, there is no substitute for the president as the principal agent in dealing with large donors. Enthusiastic and articulate members of the faculty may be of great help in fields of their interest, but the president must reflect the university's total interest in and lasting gratitude for the benefaction. With the growth of annual giving by alumni, the president's role in fund raising has been broadened. In meetings with the alumni, he is the chief channel of communications as to policy and progress and, at the same time, the most influential exponent of the virtues of thoughtful and generous support.

It is for these reasons that the president of a liberal university cannot expect his board of trustees to lift the burden of fund raising from his shoulders. Trustees can develop precious leads and valuable contacts, but in the moment of truth it is not personal relations but institutional purpose that convinces the thoughtful donor. With the pressure for funds to support the increasing needs of the liberal university today, it would be foolish to assume that fund raising will become less important in the total endeavors of a president. The development office can do a more efficient and sensitive job; the faculty can learn that fund raising is an interesting diversion; but the president remains the key to sustained success. One of the most promising sources of confidence in support of his endeavors is the steadily widening sense of responsibility shown by a large segment of the alumni.

The proliferation of departments, activities, and services has placed upon the university president a growing burden of responsibility for which he may not come prepared. This is the leadership and administration of a large supporting staff of many levels and categories of professional and administrative personnel quite apart from the faculty. The president who has come up through the faculty is accustomed to a partnership form of administration in which decision by committees and implementation by individuals of roughly equal status are customary. In staff operations, however, organization is hierarchical and supervision must be exercised through several layers of responsibility. In faculty organization, the diverse interests of members are loosely ordered by colleague opinion and the authority of ideas and professional status. In staff organization, there must be more positive direction and assignment of tasks in order to assure a well-organized team.

As universities have grown in size and complexity, the president has thus found himself more and more the chief officer of a supporting operation, distinct in structure and approach from that of the faculty but intimately related to it. Elements of this supporting organization range from admissions, aid, counseling, health services, and athletics to libraries, laboratories, research administration, and computer centers. While the financial and purely business side of the institution can be separated out for supervision by senior officers experienced in these fields, the categories of activities in close support of academic programs seem to require the integrating influence of the president in a more sustained and direct manner.

The nub of the problem for the president in dealing with a complex supporting staff is to develop a sense of organization and the art of supervision through a hierarchy of carefully selected delegates constantly schooled on mission and policy. Since a professor hesitates to tell another professor how or what to teach, a "professor-president" sometimes avoids telling an admissions officer or the director of athletics what he considers appropriate policy for the institution. But the supporting staff of a liberal university is intimately involved in the *total* mission and personality of the particular institution and is not composed of teacher-scholars whose diverse interests and approaches are averaged or balanced out in the overall educational process. Institutional policy in admissions, aid, athletics, health, discipline, counseling, and research contracts, as well as in the employment of nonfaculty supporting personnel, must be definite, understood, and implemented. Participation of many faculty or administrative committees in recommending proper policy does not relieve the president of *line* responsibility over the supporting staff which implements the policy determined. In this area of responsibility, the president is not a super-chairman of a system of freewheeling teaching departments, but an executive leader of a hierarchical supporting team.

The support staff of many universities is only now coming to be recognized as a necessary, self-conscious, and cohesive entity.

The aura of faculty status and faculty prerogatives has often thrown the support staff into the shadows. But the supporting staff of a liberal university has great influence upon the effectiveness of teaching and scholarship within an institution which seeks to educate the whole man. The sense of status, mission, and partnership of a supporting staff in a liberal university is, therefore, essential. This requires that the president, as chief executive officer in the administration of the university, must develop and utilize all the arts of organization, communications, industrial relations, and control in assuring that the supporting staff is an effective and integral element in his institution. There will always remain a degree of sensitivity in regard to the relative status, prerogatives, and rewards of the faculty and supporting staff. The president, as the chief officer of both, must resolve sensitivity into understanding to the highest degree possible.

Since the president of an institution tends to set the pattern of executive leadership in a highly sensitive, interacting type of organization, it seems appropriate to suggest certain attributes of effective administration which he may embody in his own activity and thereby encourage in others.

To allow adequate time for the consultation peculiarly necessary in academic administration, the president must learn to anticipate problems or issues so that the need for last-minute, hasty consultations and clearances can be avoided to the fullest extent possible. Academic people are more given to free discussion than to quick decision. Interested in ideas as such, they want time to consider them. The professor who becomes a president must speed up his processes of reaching decision because he has so many and such diverse decisions to make, but he cannot presume that his colleagues in the faculty have changed their tempo. Therefore, he must push back the time at which he begins his consultations on proposals for change in policies or programs, especially if these concern the faculty of his institution.

An aspect of anticipation is the art of encouraging key members of both faculty and staff to consider a range of possible developments still well in the future by informal mention apart from the immediate issue which justifies the current consultation. Much of the art of administration at the higher level is "preventive medicine," to keep responsible people from becoming cozy and comfortable in their area of operations and responsibility and to avoid errors of judgment by consideration of possible problems *before* they arise. The effective administrator maintains an informal flow of ideas downward through the organization. If the ideas find support and flow back with widening acceptance, they are the better for the journey. It is easier to gain true consensus on an idea which has circulated around the campus for weeks than for a sudden inspiration of the "boss."

It is in the nature of a university that the scope of communications be inclusive rather than exclusive. Experience has shown that it is better for a president to tell his trustees, faculty, and staff more rather than less than they need to know. Except for individual salaries, there are few items of *fact* that need to be kept confidential. On a residential type of campus, most issues of any importance are widely discussed long before decisions are made. It is better that they be debated with the facts available rather than on the basis of rumor. It is easy for executives at all levels to gain a sense of satisfaction in possessing privileged information. The satisfaction of broad support from a well-informed constituency is a much greater satisfaction. To communicate the good news and hold back the bad is both unwise and futile. There is nothing worse for morale in any organization than a loss in confidence in the reliability of official information.

The most difficult art of a chief executive is that of evaluating people. This is so much a matter of the innate qualities of the evaluator that an analysis of procedures helps but little. Sensitivity, intuition, and imagination must be balanced by disciplined objectivity and the capacity to draw upon tested experience. Suffice it to say that at the presidential level, the selection of key staff rises beyond the level of customary, formal evaluation procedures. While the fullest knowledge of past experience and accomplishments of the candidate is necessary, the decision is usually one concerning the potentialities of the person in a new position or a new environment. This involves a sensing not only of his powers in terms of specialized knowledge and skills, but of the degree of mutual reinforcement he will afford in a closely knit team. A parallel art is that of differentiating between the important and the less important in the assignment of one's effort and time. With many constituencies and the less formal climate of a campus, a president can become the slave of a personal relations syndrome. It is, of course, better to delegate the study of a problem than to delegate the persuasion of a person to one's point of view on an important issue. Where no issue is involved, visits of protocol can be kept brief. But where *both* an important problem and consultation or communication with an important person are involved, the appearance of haste is unfortunate. This is peculiarly true in dealing with key staff. It is sometimes the temptation of a tired president to spend time with "important" visitors where no issues are involved, unconsciously to avoid giving time to a dean or vice-president who needs to bring a sticky issue to resolution. It is the part of wisdom, however, to encourage such officers to transmit both their recommendations and a brief summary of considerations which lead to them, in writing, in advance. In this way the consultations with those in the higher administration in whom the president has full confidence can be expedited or, often, they can be limited to a phone call or a brief memorandum.

A further means of conserving the time of a president in consultation with his senior officers is the holding of periodic staff conferences, whether formalized by some designation or not. If these are definitely scheduled ahead, consultation on an issue involving two or more officers can await the presence of all those directly involved and of others who should be informed. Such a group discussion of policies usually brings out diverse points of view more readily than does individual consultation. It is also sometimes better to let a fellow staff member criticize a questionable proposal than for the president to do so. It is important, however, for the president to maintain the assumption that a periodic staff conference is a device of consultation and not of policy formation by vote. In such meetings the president's vote is the only one that counts, and he may reserve judgment.

It is with the younger and newer members of his immediate team that the president needs to spend more time. With these, the president must become a teacher and a coach. He must assign responsibility even to the point of risk, but still must be ready to give steadying counsel and support. He must overcome the tendency in an academic environment to delay unfavorable criticism of a younger colleague until it is too late to help. Under a well-tested concept of agency, he must stand behind his officers when their judgment falters. With a person of high potential, detailed comments on mistakes are unnecessary. An indication of continued confidence and informal suggestions on *future* strategy are the best form of preventive medicine.

With the best of insight in selection and the most patient counseling, some of any president's appointees will prove inadequate. In the environment of a university, administrative surgery needs to be somewhat more delicate and deliberate than in profit-and-loss industry, but it does not need to be as tardy as is often the case. Despite closer personal relations and more sensitive constituencies, the good of the institution and the morale of colleagues and subordinates must be balanced against the feelings of the person who has failed. The unhappy job of breaking the news to the individual should be that of the person who appointed him, the president. A helpful approach in such interviews is to relate the need for change to the interest of the staff member, his avoidance of further frustration, and his opportunity to use his particular talents to better advantage. It is best and proper to suggest that it is a lack of fit between the person and the assignment that has led to the painful decision rather than any inherent defects in the person. It is costly in terms of any individual's confidence in himself for the employer in such situations to assume the role of an omniscient judge. It is both humane and wise to sustain self-confidence rather than to impair it, whether the individual is to be transferred or he resigns. The job is to preserve effective organization and operations, not to justify one's decision to terminate in the presence of the terminee.

It was stated earlier that it is in the balanced interplay of leadership in ideas and leadership of an operating, dynamic organization that the quality of a president is tested. Yet it is the nature of human experience that most of us have more ideas than we can implement when we are young and more capacity for implementation than compelling convictions when we are old. As a president becomes experienced in administration and imbued with the satisfactions of a smoothly running institution, he may lose some of his earlier enthusiasm for change. He may become more interested in new buildings than in new educational ventures. But as a leader in an institution dealing with young people, new ideas, and new approaches in a dynamic society, he cannot permit himself to become an effective but cautious bureaucrat. It is not necessary that proposals for change originate in a president's own mind, but that he keep his mind open to the flow of suggestions which well up in his institution. It is his maturing experience in sifting out the best ideas, along with his enhanced powers in putting ideas to work in a complex, human organization, that justifies his continuance in office.

$\mathcal{S} \quad 3 \quad \mathcal{C}$

THE
FACULTY

a. The Faculty as a Corporate Body

There is much confusion in the minds of most people who have
not lived and worked within an academic community concerning
the bounds and functions of a university faculty. To many, including most students, the faculty is an amorphous collection of persons who teach, part time or full time, or have something to do
with students. From the undergraduate point of view, a teaching
assistant, a student counselor, and an assistant registrar are merged
into the role of those who influence his educational experience;

and since they are not fellow students, they are considered a part of the "faculty."

With the growth of organized research programs, another source of confusion in the demarcation of the faculty has arisen. While many professors carry on research, other professional personnel have been added to support them in their efforts. Although the line is sometimes difficult to draw, it appears best to restrict the term "faculty" to those who normally participate to some reasonable degree in organized instruction and who, by the terms of their appointment, whether on continuing tenure or term appointment, are entitled to participate in the planning of curriculum and the recommendation of students for degrees. Such a line may exclude professional librarians as well as research physicists from membership in the university faculty, but it clarifies organization to distinguish categories by specific function within the institution rather than by professional attainment. The medical director deals with students and the chief planning engineer deals with research facilities, but they are not normally members of the faculty. A university needs the contributions of many professional experts, but the core group engaged in the essential, central function of the university—teaching—seems to be the body which should be designated as "the faculty."

The university faculty as a cohesive, ongoing, policy-making body which helps to sustain the standards, values, and personality of an institution appears to have become lost in a fog of bigness on some American campuses. The forces toward atomization are great, and for many faculty members participation in organized structures and procedures is not as thrilling as research in one's specialty. Recent student protests have made clear, in some institutions, a trend which had become increasingly definite over the years. A faculty of specialists in teaching and scholarship was gradually but surely giving up by default a policy-making function which was its right and obligation.

In a liberal university in particular, the faculty as a corporate body must assume a heavy responsibility for the educational traditions and policies of the institution. In its corporate capacity, as a total faculty, it represents the unifying mechanism for bringing all knowledge, understanding, insights, and values to bear upon the manner in which succeeding generations of students and younger scholars are developed. Consisting of highly educated men and women, dedicated to an age-old profession, it must seek to uphold standards of truth, integrity, dedication, and service within itself and on the part of its institution and the disciplines it professes. The faculty of a university has some of the attributes of a medieval guild in its participation, in a large degree, in self-government, in the selection of candidates for membership, and in the determination of standards of performance. That teacher-scholars are *appointed* to membership and not *employed* on a staff is of real and not merely traditional significance. On appointment, the member joins the partnership or a complex system of partnerships. The designation of membership should therefore be definite and not casual, and the responsibilities of membership should be clear.

The usual requirement for membership in a faculty in an older university is regular appointment to one of the three established ranks of professor, associate professor, and assistant professor. In some universities, however, a distinction is made between the "tenure faculty," which usually includes the two senior ranks, and the larger group including assistant professors on term appointment. Persons on visiting appointment, lecturers, instructors, and other temporary, part-time, or junior personnel, as well as persons on research appointment without professorial designation, may be considered "officers of instruction and research" without the voting privileges of membership in the faculty.

This degree of exclusiveness seems justified by the need that a voting member of the faculty have sufficient experience and involvement in teaching and sufficient identification with the institution to warrant participation in determining its educational policies. This does not necessarily preclude the attendance of appropriate nonvoting personnel at the meetings of the voting faculty if factors of size and tradition are favorable. A broader eligibility for attendance than for voting may lessen the sharpness of distinctions and improve morale and communications without loss of a clear definition of responsibilities.

It may be necessary, on the other hand, in large universities to reduce the size of the legislative body acting for the faculty by some method of representation. The gain in avoiding a large and unwieldy assembly is offset, however, by a loss in communications from and to the general faculty. This loss may become serious in a time when critical issues require full debate by members of widely divergent views and resolution by a general consensus acceptable to the whole faculty.

Within the voting faculty, thus defined, the center of gravity usually becomes a body of members on tenure appointment with long and overlapping periods of service. It is this group that develops, over the years, a quality of mutual understanding, judgment, and concern which is a precious resource in a liberal university. A diversity of viewpoint related to discipline, level of instruction, emphasis upon research, or interest in student affairs may persist, but it is likely to be tempered in debate by mutual respect and accommodation and a common sense of responsibility.

A university is most fortunate if such a policy-making body has evolved. It cannot be brought suddenly into existence when critical issues arise. For the university and for the faculty itself, it is a long-run investment in institutional integrity and personality well worth the time required for regular meetings. Attendance may vary, but an ongoing, working assembly must exist.

As with most organizations in which diverse points of view must be brought into consensus, the social relations within a faculty, on and off campus, as well as participation in many cross-university activities, help to create a climate of institutional commitment and mutual understanding. Vigorous discussions in a faculty club provide a catharsis for more extreme points of view. Where a faculty lives near the campus, shop talk is likely to occur between members of different disciplines. The range of "extracurricular" activities of faculty members and their wives in more or less formal groups varies from institution to institution. The by-product of enhanced identity of members with an ongoing academic community is usually evident. Over time, tradition contributes to the sense of solidarity, including the participation in academic ceremonies and official receptions, and recognition on retirement or commemoration on death. Pride in an institution is built upon pride in the accomplishments of its members. The reading of a memorial minute on the death of a distinguished professor long retired affords younger members a sense of belonging to a fellowship of dedicated teacher-scholars.

It is unfortunate that growing size and the increasing dispersal of faculty residence in some institutions has reduced the social bonds which hold men of like mind and profession together. There is now increasing interest in faculty residential projects and improved faculty clubs to offset this loss in relationship. The factors of differentiation in discipline, the shift to research, and the demands of the outside world have combined to reduce the sense of community which gives a faculty, as such, its strength. Dependent upon mutual understanding and mutual reinforcement in the preservation of a great tradition of academic freedom and leadership in ideas, the faculty of a liberal university needs a sense of community as never before. A great corporation can scatter its personnel and operations over a continent. A liberal university is a far more sensitive organism. Unless this is recognized, the term "university" may become a misnomer.

b. The Faculty and the President

The relations of the faculty, as a corporate body, with the president of a liberal university are of great importance to the welfare of the institution. As leader of the faculty, the president should preside at meetings of the faculty, not as a passive moderator, but as an active participant. While freedom and good order in discussion require observance of parliamentary procedure, it is helpful for the president to have the right of comment without the formality of leaving the chair. Many of the problems coming before a faculty involve interrelations with the other constituencies which the president must respect. Further, many of the policies determined as beneficial by the faculty must be implemented through administrative officers responsible to the president, as such, even though working in close cooperation with appropriate faculty committees. The faculty may approve a new policy or program, but the president and his appointees must put it into effect. There needs to be understanding from the first as to what it is possible to implement. In the resolution of such accommodation, the deans are valuable contributors, but the essential relationship is between the president and the faculty as a corporate body.

The relations between the president and the faculty are strengthened by many scheduled or casual meetings apart from the general meetings of the faculty. In addition to his meetings with deans and other administrative officers, the president's conferences with chairmen of departments, directors of programs, and faculty members assigned to ad hoc missions in planning new ventures, raising funds, or dealing with outside bodies constitute an ongoing flow of interchange. But the president must also recognize the traditional attitude of *all* faculty members that they are colleagues and not employees. This involves a readiness to meet with any individual faculty member or group of members who have a grievance or a pressing personal need. The president is in a position of last resort when a faculty member is disturbed by either the decisions of his colleagues or serious personal problems. While there must be a respect for normal channels of appeal and close coordination with those to whom responsibility has been delegated, the president of a university cannot assume the degree of hierarchical aloofness which protects the senior officer of a large corporation. At the same time, direct access to the president should not become the privilege of a favored few from among those not in an official position involving such access.

It has been found in some institutions that a supplementary channel of communications between the faculty and the president, apart from that through deans, departmental chairmen, and functional committees, provides a useful means of keeping the president aware of faculty opinion. Such a channel may be an elected advisory committee on general policy which meets with the president at his request or on the committee's initiative. The establishment of such a committee involves some risk if it is permitted to infringe upon the jurisdiction of faculty committees of long-established function or to become a "watchdog" committee on deans. The essential function of such a committee on general policy is to communicate ideas and reactions through discussion with the president, and not to make independent investigations and reports. When an idea appeals to the president, the study of its value and feasibility should be assigned through normal channels within the administration or the general committee structure. The warp and woof of faculty relations with a president are in his day-to-day role in administering a complex operation under existing policy rather than in the development of new policies. Conferences relate to a multitude of specific matters, such as departmental plans, appointments, finances, facilities, fund raising, research programs, and interdepartmental cooperation. Personal relations in dealing with a constant stream of such practical business develop mutual understanding of views and temperaments and provide a foundation for the mutual respect needed when major issues of universitywide policy arise. It would be the fortunate president who could give pleasing response to even a majority of the specific proposals coming over his desk, particularly those involving appointments and appropriations. A faculty, in its more thoughtful moments, realizes that this must be so, although conviction runs high in the dedicated scholar. In the longer run, the lasting source of goodwill in administrative relations is confidence in the integrity, impartiality, and sympathetic concern of the man who must assume final responsibility.

A potential source of conflict between a faculty and a president arises in divergent judgments concerning the pace and direction of innovation. The need for anticipation, communication, and participation in the approach to change has been discussed. But universities are competitive, and presidents may be more aware of changing conditions than a faculty carrying on its teaching and scholarship in comfortable isolation. The president must judge the shifting consensus of his faculty as new ideas are discussed. Serious friction occurs when, through haste, oversight, or frustration, a president commits his institution to an educational policy or project without prior or sufficient consultation with his faculty.

On the other hand, a faculty which assumes prerogatives beyond its power or its competency to judge wisely corrodes the essential leadership which permits the university to meet new conditions. The present situation in many European universities is the result of a traditional concentration of power in the faculty. The faculties of some American universities have sometimes forgotten that a legislative body needs sustained leadership, not within itself alone, but in the hands of one who is responsible for the university as a whole, over time, and in the face of external forces. Increasingly, in the private, liberal university, the economy of the institution requires understanding accommodation between the body which is primarily concerned with academic policy and the president who is also responsible for its effective support and execution. This need is so great that oversensitivity concerning precise prerogatives, and, especially, the carrying on of emotional debates about them have come to be an expensive luxury in the administration of a complex institution.

c. The Faculty and the Trustees

The relations between the faculty and a board of trustees, while far less close than those between the faculty and a president, can be both constructive and rewarding. There appears to be a basic principle for continuing success, however; this is that both groups respect the important rule that proposals with respect to policy in the administration of the university should be channeled *through* the president in both the downward and the upward direction. An outside member of a business board of directors would be foolish to interfere in company management. A board member who meddles in university operations is making the same mistake. Likewise, a dean or professor who seeks to go around the president in influencing board actions is not only planting the seeds of trouble but is undermining the vital separation and balance between faculty responsibilities and board responsibilities. The trustee who may be influenced through such devious channels might in turn seek to influence faculty decisions in the faculty's proper sphere of initiative. A president is in a far stronger position to represent and defend faculty interests before the board if his position has not been weakened by a resort to special pleading by individual faculty members or groups.

This does not mean that a wall of silence need be built between the board of trustees and the faculty as a group. Rather, it is highly advantageous that respected and responsible channels be arranged for a continuing flow of information from the faculty to the board concerning the academic life of the university. One method is to have representative faculty members engage in informal discussions on their field of interest at periodic dinner sessions with the appropriate trustee committee or the full board. Another is to co-opt members of the board to attend the annual meetings of departmental advisory councils. Faculty lectures and seminars for alumni normally include board members in the audience. The aim is to provide the board with as rich an understanding of the intellectual life of the university as possible in order to make the mission of the university both clear and challenging. Board members become weary of financial and business responsibilities unless refreshed by contact with the true business of the university—the advancement of knowledge and the education of young people.

A somewhat more formal arrangement for communication between the faculty and the board of trustees is the election by the faculty of a "committee on conference." Ideally, such a committee should be small, with perhaps six members elected on a rotating basis for three year terms. In one institution, such a faculty committee meets with the "curriculum" or educational committee of the board four times a year at dinner after the regular meeting of the latter committee. Each time, the faculty committee provides a program on some aspect of university life, calling upon faculty specialists as panelists to lead the discussions. Subjects include the various disciplines covered in the university, new frontiers in research, new methods of instruction, and other educational concerns of the faculty. Problems of an administrative nature are avoided. Once a year the faculty committee on conference joins with the full board in serving as host at dinner for all academic officers, chairmen of departments, and the members of standing committees of the faculty.

An exception to the emphasis upon intellectual rather than administrative matters in faculty-board contacts may well be made in the case of appeals against the president's decision in a question of tenure or other personal grievance. Even though cases may seldom arise, a growing understanding of sound industrial relations suggests that there should be an established procedure whereby an individual faculty member can appeal to the board as the legally responsible entity, against what he feels to be a failure on the part of the president to fulfill a contract or a presumed contract. There should exist an elected, standing committee of the faculty which, after hearing the faculty member, can sit with a standing committee of the board to consider the case. To give such a faculty committee a continuing function in the hopefully long interval between appeals, it may serve also as the committee on conference suggested above. In this way the committee on conference, while building rapport with the board of trustees as a continuing source of information on educational developments, becomes an effective channel for the discussion of faculty grievances whenever these arise.

Another obvious exception to the principle of channeling formal relations between the board and the faculty through the president is the use of a faculty committee to consult with the board in the selection of a new president. The selection of a president is one of the most important functions that a board of trustees performs. It is peculiarly the board's responsibility. But a board is most unwise if, in an institution highly dependent upon response to leadership rather than upon command, it does not effectively canvass the views of those who can best anticipate likely response.

d. The Faculty as a Means of Institutional Integration

While faculty relations with the president and the board of trustees are important determinants of effective organization in a liberal university, the test of the contribution of a faculty as a corporate body is whether it can develop and sustain a well-integrated system of academic policies and standards. Over time, a faculty can determine whether an institution is a liberal university or a system of job shops. With a wide diversity of subject specializations within the faculty, the forces toward atomization and disintegration are constantly at work. Increased emphasis upon specialized graduate instruction and organized research increases the centrifugal pressures. Yet a liberal university has the obligation to maintain its focus upon the development of liberally educated persons of high talent and upon the integration of knowledge as well as its extension at the periphery. The balancing of the forces toward specialization and academic disintegration and the counterpressures toward integration is the most essential and yet the most difficult function of the faculty as a corporate body. Fortunately, there are several attributes and devices which help on the side of integration in a university which seeks to preserve a liberal tradition.

Probably the most effective factor in preserving integration is the wholehearted support by the faculty of the principle that the undergraduate college continues to be the central, traditional core and responsibility of a liberal university. So long as a large proportion of the faculty is active in and concerned with undergraduate education as a whole, there is more likelihood that the educational program will remain man-centered rather than becoming knowledge-centered. The focus on the student will of itself support to some degree the concept that knowledge is a *means* to education rather than its end and, secondarily, that new knowledge is more significant as it becomes integrated with an older and broader base of knowledge.

It is for this reason that the university which permits or encourages the specialization of its faculty, more particularly in arts and sciences, that divides it up into those who teach undergraduates and those who teach only graduate students, loses a vital factor in sustaining its academic integrity as a liberal university. Personal prestige, economy of effort, and overemphasis on research may lead the individual faculty member to avoid undergraduate teaching. Departmental or institutional ambitions to secure men of distinction may lead to exemptions from undergraduate instruction. But the influence of the faculty as a body in sustaining a presumption and pattern of balanced interest can do much to offset individual, departmental, or institutional temptations to discount the need for the integrating effect of widespread participation in the central-core function of the university, the undergraduate college. It is true that the influence of the faculty is exercised mainly through community attitudes and individual example, but there are also more specific means of implementing such assumptions through the policies of committees reporting to the faculty.

One mechanism useful in implementing a faculty policy favoring academic integration is the faculty committee on the undergraduate course of study. This committee should have the right to review courses in terms of number, degree of specialization, level of requirement, and method of instruction. With the support and leadership of the appropriate dean, it can question the department which permits undergraduate courses to become split up into bits and pieces of subject matter taught by junior faculty over against more balanced and integrated courses requiring the mature understanding of senior men. Younger instructors are ambitious to have courses of their own in their chosen specialty and may become restless if this privilege is long delayed. But it is the responsibility of the faculty in a liberal university as a corporate body to maintain control of the educational process and not permit a drift toward easy tolerance for the interests of younger—or older—specialists who prefer the dispensing of knowledge to the far harder task of truly educating young persons.

Another means of implementing a faculty policy favoring academic integration is the development of an effective faculty advisory committee on appointments. Such a committee, dealing with appointments or promotions in the more senior ranks, should be representative of the several divisions of the university and thereby serve to counterbalance the tendency of some departments to move away from undergraduate teaching toward graduate specialization, or from teaching as a whole toward research. Since the members from other divisions are not experts in the field of the candidate for appointment or promotion, they should be more ready to question his overall interest and effectiveness in teaching and in the general educational program of the department and the university. Such an advisory committee comes to have the function of influencing the character of the institution by the most effective process of all, the determination of who shall become a part of the faculty of the future. It is a wise president or dean who keeps this function evident in the deliberations of such an advisory committee.

In the control of the number and nature of courses and in the qualifications and interests of new entrants to the tenure ranks, the faculties of most universities today are subject to an increasing pressure for economy. While the need for economy in offerings and appointments may become discouraging for the particular department, it is at the same time a wholesome stimulus to more careful planning. This, of itself, should lead to a more integrated structure in curriculum and a better balance in faculty interests. As in all arts, the need for economy tends to improve the quality and integrity of the product. In the art of academic administration, the need for economy should, if understood by even the most ambitious faculty, have the same effect.

The presence of a need for economy involves a delicate balance between those elements in a university which are responsible for financing—primarily, the trustees and the financial officers—and those who are concerned with the improvement and extension of instruction and scholarship—primarily, the faculty. The president and his immediate staff—the deans—stand in the middle. A rigid and inelastic control of academic operations by the financial side leads to a disheartened faculty. An arbitrary and ever-demanding faculty leads to an irritated and stubborn board and treasury staff. The avoidance of either extreme has come to be an important aim in university operations today. While measures to attain this end will be discussed later, it is noted at this point because it involves the interest and obligation of the faculty in a liberal university, as a corporate body, to sustain the forces toward institutional integration at a time when opposing pressures are strong.

e. The Committee Structure of a Faculty

There is usually much talk in faculty circles of the time wasted in meetings of universitywide committees. Some faculty members would prefer to restrict their concerns to those of their department and discipline. This, again, reflects the centrifugal forces at work in a time of specialization. Other faculty members are both interested and effective in the integrating elements of institutional policy and operations, the central committees. Four of these universitywide committees have already been mentioned: a committee on the undergraduate course of study, an advisory committee on faculty appointments and advancements, a committee on general policy advisory to the president, and a committee on conference with the trustees.

Long experience supports a position of restraint in determining the extent to which the committee structure of a faculty is allowed to proliferate. Most faculties have too many committees. Yet, if there were not committees to cooperate with the administration in the consideration of educational policy, curriculum, admissions, appointments and promotions, and the library, even the most aloof member would become aroused at the loss of faculty prerogatives, especially when his own department or his own students were affected. On the other hand, some faculty members would like to avoid any participation in dealing with student discipline, athletics, or extracurricular activities, overlooking the basic premise that liberal education affects the whole man and that the attitude, manners, enthusiasm, and general tone of a student in class are a reflection of his total environment. There appears to be no precise test of how many faculty committees there should be except the pragmatic one of what policies and operations over the years *should* and *will* concern the faculty sufficiently to assure a worthwhile meeting of appropriate length at appropriate intervals. A faculty which abrogates its proper role as participant or adviser in policy determination or implementation in a significant area of academic life and then rends its corporate garments when trouble comes is not a good example of the maturity it seeks to inculcate in its students.

Committees are essential in organizations dependent upon response rather than command in their effective operation. There are, perhaps, only three types of faculty committees which are worth the time they take: advisory, legislative, and quasi-judicial.

An advisory committee should not legislate, and a legislative committee should not judge individual cases. An advisory committee helps the president or other executive in communicating attitudes or suggestions for change in policies or operations and should meet with the administrator involved rather than apart from him. A legislative committee helps to formulate policy into law acceptable to the faculty. A quasi-judicial committee interprets law, policy, and standards in specific cases. All afford a spread of participation and consultation. A committee without specific business, sustained leadership, and adequate staff support is a waste of time. It is such committees which stimulate justifiable complaints from the busier members of the faculty although affording an excuse for others to avoid more arduous duties.

Experience indicates that, for most purposes, small committees are more effective than large committees. A committee of seven members of whom six, other than the chairman, are elected by the faculty as a whole appears to work well. An ideal upper limit might be ten. But the limited size and the method of selection enhance the sense of responsibility, the institutionwide concern, and the ability to gain consensus within the committee. The least effective committee is one for which each department or school nominates a faculty member. Not only can such a committee become too large for effective discussion and consensus on difficult issues, but it tends to emphasize departmental attitudes rather than best universitywide policy. A small committee can hold hearings to make sure that the interests and opinions of all departments are adequately represented; it is expensive in time and energy to have all the "witnesses" present in the committee itself. Further, large representative committees undermine the concept that a university committee is an agency of the faculty as a corporate body rather than of the departments. To assure breadth of understanding, however, the membership of the smaller type of faculty committee should, by rule, include professors from the major divisions of the university.

While experience differs among universities with respect to the focus of leadership in faculty committees, it appears increasingly evident that most committees function best if chaired by an appropriate academic officer rather than by a professor. There are several reasons for this: First, there is the fact, already mentioned with respect to the president, that the academic officer will be the person who implements the policy or decision and should, therefore, be in a position to assure a thorough canvassing of the problems and repercussions which might arise. The faculty member, while a part of management in many respects, is not usually in a position to anticipate problems outside his own area of experience. Second, the academic officer should have the time and staff to develop clear-cut agendas for meetings and the information needed for decision. He is also in a better position to keep discussion on the track and to avoid time-consuming debates as to facts rather than principles. Third, an academic officer can emphasize a universitywide approach to problems and can lift deliberations above the level of interdepartmental logrolling. This, again, is a factor in preserving the concept of an integrated academic structure through sustained leadership, rather than permitting policy making to drift into merely mediation between diverse interests.

The academic officer chairing a faculty committee must, however, retain the attitude that he is a member of the faculty assisting his colleagues to reach wise conclusions. If he gives the slightest impression that he is omniscient and that he looks upon a committee meeting as either a rubber-stamp operation or a necessary but time-consuming interruption in a busy day, the climate for cooperative administration deteriorates. The interplay of faculty opinion and judgment and administrative judgment and execution in a liberal university is a very delicate and sensitive factor and yet vital to wholesome change and growth. Effective guidance of such interplay requires well-considered experience and penetrating understanding on the part of the academic officer. It is probably the reason why most successful presidents and deans have been professors for a part of their careers. It appears wasteful to divert a creative teacher-scholar into academic administration, but the need for subtle understanding in this very sensitive area of university operation seems to justify the practice. An "efficient" professional executive without professorial experience can create cleavage and antagonism despite the best of intentions. The operations of a faculty committee involve *both* policy development and institutional "industrial" relations.

It is assumed that the academic officer who has chaired a faculty committee will report its findings or recommendations to the general faculty. In this he is acting as the committee spokesman and not, primarily, as an officer of administration. If he is unsuccessful in securing the approval of the faculty, even with the help of his committee, it is the committee which is rebuffed, not the administration alone. While this fact is not always clear, it is wise to make it evident in order to enhance the sense of managerial responsibility of both the faculty and the committee. The committee is an arm of the faculty as a corporate body, and not merely a group of consultants to the academic officer.

There is, however, at least one exception to the wise practice of having academic officers act as chairmen of faculty committees. This is the faculty committee on conference with the board of trustees discussed earlier with respect to relations with the board. As an elected committee, carefully designed to be a "safety valve" and a judicial body in communicating faculty opinion to the board, in general or in cases of individual grievance, it is well to provide that it elect its own chairman from outside the administration. The university which establishes this mechanism within its normal faculty structure will avoid the pressure for ad hoc or unofficial committees should differences arise. The chairmanship of such a conference committee should rotate with the changing membership of the committee. Chairmanship, as well as membership, on such a committee should be a recognized aspect of *faculty* activity *within* the university, and not as an outside endeavor.

f. The Departmental Structure of a Faculty

The "workhorse" unit in faculty organization in a liberal university is the department. The term "department" can be applied, for economy in discussion, to any school or program which acts as a department in being the instrument for the initiation and implementation of policy concerning curriculum and instruction within its defined area, for the initiation of recommendations concerning professional personnel, and for the immediate oversight of instructional and research activities in its field. The department plans, recommends, and operates within a framework of policies and procedures established by the university as a whole. It is the device which has evolved in American universities to permit close and effective leadership and control in many highly diverse and demanding programs of instruction and scholarship within the context of a unifying university structure. It provides the differentiating force which, balanced against and yet in combination with the integrating pressures of university purposes and policies, gives vigor and flexibility to a complex institution. In general, it was and remains a most necessary and successful invention. Like all "federal" devices in government, however, it creates tensions which must be resolved constructively.

In more recent years, the effectiveness of the department as a unit of organization and administration has become counterbalanced in some degree by its limitations in adjusting to the rapid changes which have occurred in the coverage and interrelations of instruction and scholarship within the university. Human knowledge has always been an expanding universe without neat, definable subdivisions. In simpler times, however, the central core of the discipline called "physics," for example, was quite distinct from that of chemistry. But now, with a vast expansion of the frontiers of research, there has come to be a subfield called "physical chemistry" and another called "chemical physics." One can list many new hybrids, such as biochemistry, geophysics, astrophysics, mathematical economics, behavioral politics, economic history, and social anthropology. New fields which run across older departmental lines add to the problem of keeping faculty organization, on the one hand, and instruction and scholarship, on the other, in some workable coordination. It is enough to list linguistics, comparative literature, industrial relations, public affairs, regional and urban studies, and the history of science and philosophy. Contrary to the old notions that hybrids are sterile and that cross-disciplinary projects are superficial, some of the most exciting and creative work in the university is being carried on in areas and combinations of areas never contemplated when departmental jurisdictions became established.

It would be fortunate if departments as organizations of people could be as responsive to change and interaction as freely moving scholarship, but this is too much to expect. New ventures between disciplines and across disciplines are likely to be considered suspect by the older, more conservative members of a department. Budgets, new appointments, new courses, and a shift in enrollments are involved. So long as a professor's salary and promotion, the courses he teaches, the fellowships available to his graduate students, and the facilities and services he uses are within the control of his "home" department, there is likely to be some sense of restraint upon his forays afield.

To offset the restraining influence of departmental organization upon the changing directions of academic enterprise, most universities have established a varied range of supplementary mechanisms. These include: interdepartmental programs with separate budgets, with or without the authority to recommend appointments; research units with separate budgets to permit the purchase of faculty time; approved combinations of graduate studies with an interdepartmental committee authorized to recommend students for fellowships and degrees; and many others. The last step in such an adjustment to change is the establishment of a new department or school. The critical factors in the decision are the viability of the new area as a "discipline" or, at least, a cohesive, integrated, educational enterprise; the number of faculty members and students involved; the quality of leadership; and the availability of special funds. Educational objections to the too ready establishment of additional, more specialized departments are, however, reinforced by the normal expectation that a new department will cost much more in the years ahead than a less formal and self-conscious unit in university organization.

Just as a university faculty as a whole must develop a corporate consciousness, so a good department must mature into something more than the sum of its parts. This, again, requires effective leadership, good communications, and accepted tradition. In academic circles, the personality and standing of a department become, over time, almost as distinctive as the personality and standing of a university. Pride in a department is a vital element in pride in an institution as a whole. The wise university administrator strives to encourage such reinforcement and to avoid dichotomy.

There are many practical facets in departmental organization, such as the levels of participation in various decisions, the degree of formality in written bylaws, the frequency of meetings, committee structure, and the control over teaching assignments, leaves, office space, libraries, and laboratories. While the central university properly lays down procedures for the handling of sensitive matters such as the recommendation of new courses, appointments, promotions, and salary adjustments, it is generally wise to give departments as much freedom as possible in developing their own way of life. This is in part justified by the diversity of problems and operations in the several disciplines. It is also a means of affording greater range for responsible yet flexible initiative to a body of members who are a part of academic management.

There are, however, certain issues in departmental organization which deserve attention. Among these is the question of whether the chairman of a department should be appointed by the president or should be elected by the members of the department. Practice varies among American universities. On balance, appointment by the president, after such consultation as he deems appropriate, appears to be the better alternative, especially in the face of dynamic change. *First,* the chairman often needs the added authority which arises from being the appointee of the president in his responsibility for funds, structures, and other resources in a time when these are growing apace. *Second,* the chairmanship of a large department has come to involve onerous duties which, while necessary, are not desired by some of those best fitted to perform them. It is easier to avoid election by one's peers than to refuse appointment by one's president. The health of the department and the university may require the president not only to select the appropriate candidate but also to persuade him to serve. *Third,* the election of departmental chairmen appears to increase rather than attenuate the centrifugal forces in university organization: between those in the various subareas of a discipline; between those concerned with different levels of instruction or with teaching on the one hand and research on the other; or between those favorable to general university policy and those who are less enthusiastic. *Fourth,* especially when a department is suffering from heavy attrition by retirement or resignations or is failing to meet new challenges, the president needs the freedom to select new leadership without dependence upon the very persons who have failed to sustain momentum. The president, as a leader in an organization dependent upon response, should have the freedom to select his own subleaders. He is not dealing with a semi-autonomous town meeting, but with an essential segment of a unified structure.

Related to the question of appointment versus election of departmental chairmen is that of their term and rotation in office. Again, experience varies, even in a single institution. The duties of the office are becoming more and more arduous because of competition for personnel, changing curriculum and methods of instruction, increased enrollments, and extended research operations. The demands of rapidly developing fields encourage able and dedicated teacher-scholars to avoid long commitments to administration. For this reason, it is probable that better candidates for chairmanships are available if terms in office are kept short— for example, to a length of from three to not more than five years. The existence of a stated term of three years permits the president to correct errors in selection with limited embarrassment. It is true, however, that the increasing complexity of the chairman's job encourages longer continuance in office. There is danger, however, that the individual will become too much a professional administrator at the expense of his own development as a teacher-scholar and that his colleagues will tend to "let George do it."

On balance, it appears best to hold to rotation in office of chairmen even at the expense of time used in administrative guidance and of the normal risk of change. Senior members of a department, if at all qualified, should participate in university administration to reinforce the concept of cooperative management.

Further, styles and interests in leadership vary, and a change, even when equally able persons are involved, may of itself encourage flexibility and enterprise. Rotation may uncover a growing coziness and inertia in a department which has asked for too little or has sought comfortable accommodation rather than dynamic progress. A longtime chairman may relieve a dean of worries at the expense of gradual deterioration of departmental effectiveness.

With rotation of chairmen, a university should buttress the office, so far as is possible, with nonfaculty administrative support, especially in large departments or those with extensive laboratories and research programs. To avoid the "professional," long-continuing chairman, the central administration must provide the support of a semiprofessional or even a professional department administrative assistant. This is a growing necessity in many universities today as their faculties improve in quality and creativity and as salaries rise accordingly. It involves sound economy in the use of scarce talent. There is an increasing role for a new academic specialist, the departmental administrator. He, unlike the president or dean, does not need to come out of the professorial ranks; but with patient understanding of the needs of teacher-scholars of a given field, he can relieve them of many administrative duties in respect to budgets, staff personnel, laboratory operations, and research contracts, as well as assume immediate supervision of the "housekeeping" operations concerned with instruction. Since it is a new kind of academic position, promising candidates for such supporting assignments are not easy to find. The problems of developing supporting staff in general, which will be discussed later, are especially evident in this aspect of departmental operations.

4

THE
ADMINISTRATION

a. The Enlarging Role of the Administrative Staff

It has been said that the cutting edge of a university is the faculty and that the handle of the knife is the administration. The analogy is not farfetched. A good knife must have balance and both a keen blade and a sturdy and well-formed handle.

The ratio of manpower in the supporting administrative staff to the teaching faculty has increased steadily over the years in most, if not all, universities. In the colonial college, the president did most of the administrative work in keeping the college going. For some casual observers of the university scene, the growth in the number of academic officers, offices, and staff is a subject for caustic humor. The multiplication of deans appears to be particularly amusing. The critics of change are seldom willing to make a comparative analysis of what has happened over the years in their own business or profession.

The university, and especially the liberal university, which concerns itself with the whole man and the integration as well as the extension of knowledge, employs very scarce talent at every level, from beginning instructor to senior professor. In some special fields there may be but a score of mature and able teacher-scholars in the universities throughout the world. To ask such a person to spend time in routine academic housekeeping would be similar to asking a Rembrandt to paint a barn. Making room assignments or ordering laboratory supplies may be essential for orderly instruction, but the best use of scarce talent and time suggests that such necessary operations be performed by persons without years of specialized postgraduate education. On the other hand, ancillary professions and occupations which specialize in student health, counseling, food services, institutional accounting, purchasing, fund raising, and library operations, among many others, have developed to a point where a professor, though brilliant in his field, is an amateur by comparison. Division of labor in higher education has proceeded with respect to function as well as to subject. If properly planned, it is both economical and efficient.

With understandable bias, many people consider "overhead costs" as something to be deplored. A president of a distinguished university once remarked, however, that he had long been worried about the growth in the ratio of overhead costs to teaching salaries until he discovered that the best universities had the highest ratios. In simple terms, their faculties were of such quality that they warranted adequate support to avoid a wastage of talent for services best assigned to others. It is evident that the test of efficiency does not lie in accountants' figures but in an institution's effectiveness in education and scholarship. It is true that the latter is far harder to demonstrate in an annual report.

More worrisome to university executives than external criticism of mounting administrative costs is the fact that recruiting qualified personnel for the administrative support of a faculty is more difficult because of the relative visibility and distinction of faculty membership. The title "professor" has earned very real respect despite occasional misuse. The title "director of admissions" or "vice-president for development" has still to gain proper recognition in academic and lay circles. Because professors assume that they *are* the "first-class citizens" of academia, members of the supporting staff sometimes too readily accept the role of "second-class citizenship." The lag in raising staff salaries at a time of scarcity of academic personnel has not helped.

The effective progress of American universities in the coming years depends as much on the recruitment, development, and organization of highly competent and dedicated administrative staffs as on the development of strong faculties. Both require time and insight to attain. But the building of the framing organization will be more difficult because its importance has not yet been fully recognized by the other elements of the university—including the trustees, faculty, and alumni—or by the staff members themselves. The supporting professions and specialized occupations in academic enterprise need to gain the status of other dedicated and demanding callings. This will require sustained effort on the part of the universities which employ them.

b. The Administration of Educational Policies, Personnel, and Operations

The earliest academic administrative functions to become differentiated from that of the president of American colleges were those of the librarian and the registrar. The office of dean came later. At first a general deputy relieving the president of a wide range of operating functions concerned with education and student life, the dean in the modern university has become differentiated into a complex of general officers overseeing universitywide academic policies and operations and other officers overseeing particular subject areas or schools.

To provide for orderly administration and to reduce the span of control of the president to a reasonable dimension, most universities assign senior status to a provost or dean of the faculty who serves as a coordinator of educational policies and faculty appointments. The precise position and functions of the senior educational officer under the president vary considerably among universities, and whether the incumbent is a "provost," a "dean of the faculty," a "dean of arts and sciences," or something else, the degree of influence he acquires in dealing with his president and his official colleagues depends more on his attributes as an individual than on his precise title. Private, liberal universities with a strong emphasis upon the undergraduate college and upon the fundamental arts and sciences tend to enlarge the influence of the chief educational officer with respect to curriculum and appointments, whereas highly differentiated state universities emphasize his role as a coordinator of academic budgets.

There is little profit in analyzing the diverse administrative structures of American universities. Experience indicates that in no area of organization does practice depart more fully from schematic charts. The nearer one gets to the central "power structure" of the university and the farther one moves from a distinct professional school, the more one finds that individuals, and not written job descriptions, determine influence. Much depends upon the degree to which a senior officer, with the approval of his president, assumes a sense of inclusive rather than limited responsibility in the chain of communications, both downward and upward. In an institution where jurisdictional lines are not rigid and where policy decisions must be sensitive to response, the person who is widely and well informed is likely to have sustained influence on policy. Likewise the officer who knows both the intent of policy determinations and the diverse problems in implementing policy in different parts of the university, and who is ready and willing to give mature counsel to fellow deans, chairmen, and others, gains the authority of wisdom and shared responsibility. Effectiveness in guiding the interplay of leadership and response thus creates more authority than formal status. Given the character of a liberal university, in particular, this is an asset rather than a liability, even though business executives may shudder in dismay.

There are, however, common problems and issues which arise in most universities in the functioning of the upper echelons of academic administration. Some have already been suggested in the discussion of the faculty. A number of further issues can be weighed.

With the increasing burden and complexity of academic administrative duties, what should be the source and preparation for academic deans and their assistants? How far should manning the positions in the office of a senior or functional dean be dependent upon diverting creative teacher-scholars into university administration at the loss of their productivity in their special fields?

There is probably no effective substitute for the professor-trained dean for the principal holder of the office. Dealing daily with teacher-scholars imbued with the temperament and attitudes of professors, he must understand the professorial mind. Even if a highly intelligent and sensitive administrator without a background of teaching and scholarship could fill the role efficiently, for some colleagues his ability "to meet a payroll" would be no substitute for lack of proven ability "to meet a class." With the delicate interplay of faculty-administration initiative and response in academic management and the need for a full understanding of both individual and institutional goals in teaching and scholarship, it appears to be both necessary and sound to sustain the tradition of the teacher-scholar dean, at least at the senior level.

The diversion of able teacher-scholars to deaning is all the more costly, however, because complexity of duties, stability of leadership, and the need for slowly developing rapport with scores of coordinate deans and departmental chairmen tend to justify extended terms in office. If departmental chairmen rotate in office every three to five years, the dean, who must act as a teacher and coach for each new incumbent, should rotate at a much slower rate, if at all. An academic dean's chief asset is his knowledge of his senior colleagues throughout the university, as fellow administrators or as teacher-scholars. There may be more loss in effectiveness in too-frequent turnovers of academic deans than in too-frequent changes in any other university office, except perhaps in the presidency.

Yet a senior dean can remain in office so long that he loses the professorial touch. Perhaps it is better that he should come to think like a dean. Solemn pledges to continue part-time teaching are hard to fulfill. Scholarship tends to settle down into reworking old ideas or becomes replaced by essays on education or speeches to alumni. A workable device to keep the older dean alive to faculty interests and attitudes, and especially those of the younger faculty, is to provide him with two or more part-time associate deans who do rotate from full-time teaching to administration and back again to full-time teaching. Such associate deans can be assigned to handling a mass of duties not directly related to tenure appointments or promotions, major curricular changes, or delicate personal problems of older colleagues requiring more experienced judgment. At the same time, if brought into policy discussions frequently, they can make valuable contributions to wisdom in policy formation in anticipating the response of those who must implement policy. Further, the flow of younger professors through the several central academic offices adds to the numbers in the faculty who have some understanding of universitywide problems. The period in office of an associate dean might be three years, with a paid leave for recouping scholarly progress in the fourth year.

Some segments of the duties of a senior dean in a modern university require more specialized knowledge and more consistent performance than the rotating associate deans, drawn from teaching, can provide. It appears that such duties are best assigned to a full-time *assistant* dean drawn, not from the faculty, but rather from a developing academic "civil service." Such an assistant dean can help greatly in the administration of nonteaching professional personnel, such as those in research, library, museum, and computer services, whose duties are closely associated with instruction. He can also help maintain the statistical records needed for both policy development and administrative control. He becomes an accountant of academic manpower resources and utilization in a business where talent is more significant than dollars. By dividing functions which involve less directly the mutual interplay of professorial-administrative initiative and response, there can be some economy in the diversion of teacher-scholar talent.

Another practical issue in the administrative approach of a senior academic dean is the extent to which he should act as a representative of the board of trustees and the president and how far as a representative of the faculty. In the terms of university bylaws and organization charts, the dean is a line officer representing "management." An industrial executive would assume this to be evident. But in the way of life of universities, a dean would lose influence and effectiveness if he did not also act as the interpreter of faculty opinions, interests, and aspirations to the president and the board. In general, he should be sensitive to diverse faculty reactions and prepared to express his findings concerning them with clarity and understanding. In particular, he should be ready to listen sympathetically to the grievances or problems of any individual faculty member and seek to correct any injustice or help to solve any personal problem. It is in this way that he gains over time the response necessary to make his leadership effective in an organization in which the authority of status is limited. This is but a special example of a general concept of effective leadership in any human organization, but it is of peculiar importance where management is so widely shared with those who are also the subjects of management.

With respect to the proper fulfillment of contract by his colleagues on the faculty, the dean must clearly represent the board of trustees with whom that contract, written or unwritten, is made. The payment of a salary implies the rendering of service at proper times and with appropriate professional dedication. Academic accommodation does not relieve a dean of the duty of enforcing the requirement that classes be met and that university regulations be observed. Developing the assumption of a tight ship prevents a progressive sloppiness in performance.

Leadership in any human organization requires interest in individuals as well as concern for goals and the policies needed to attain them. In his interest in individuals, a senior academic officer must assist the chairmen in making sure that the personal problems of individuals which are of proper concern to the university are given attention. Such problems may include those of the physical or mental health of the faculty member or his family, serious financial difficulties, or inadequate housing. They may also involve an individual's inability or unwillingness to adjust to the standards of personal behavior assumed by his colleagues and the institution to be normal in an academic environment. In assuring that either appropriate help or justified censure is forthcoming, a dean of faculty must advise and support his chairmen. As a senior line officer, he is responsible for the morale of his constituency in *all* its aspects. There are many special conditions which surround any disciplinary action, especially where tenure is involved. These will be discussed later. But within the full range of personal help and personal correction, apart from such drastic action as termination, there are many ways to enhance a sense of membership in a mutually concerned and a mutually responsible community.

Since the problems here outlined are uniquely personal, they involve a wide range of solutions. The decision of whether to work through the chairmen, to assume direct responsibility, or to consult with the president, a member's colleague, or the medical director is a matter of judgment in each case. As time passes, a dean builds up a mental file of tested ways to help a person in trouble. These may include little-understood provisions in benefit plans, help from the president's discretionary fund, special leave arrangements, or referral to an experienced family counselor, an understanding doctor, a cooperative banker, or a wise lawyer. With all the help that a comprehensive benefit program can provide in financial terms, the critical influence upon morale in any organization is the way that organization helps the individual in solving his particular problem. No organization should appreciate this fact more than a liberal university.

c. The Control of Faculty Manpower and Utilization

With increasing pressures for economy in the operation of an institution geared to a high ratio of faculty to student enrollments, the educational administrator concerned with faculty manpower, curriculum, and methods of instruction must concentrate much of his effort upon the control of manpower and manpower utilization. With rising salaries, proliferating courses, and the constant desire of the faculty for costly seminars and other intensive devices of instruction, the task of control is both difficult and, often, thankless. But this aspect of academic management is now a vital test of survival for an operation which does not involve the economies of mass production but must meet the expectations of a faculty and staff living in a society where salaries in most other activities reflect the rising productivity resulting from mass production.

To control manpower utilization in instruction, the administrator must assure a feedback of reporting for every teaching hour used in every course or in any form of service related to instruction or scholarship. While overall controls must be in terms of dollar budgets, it has been found that a sensitive and readily available administrative instrument is that of measuring costs, in the first instance, by teaching hours.

There are many reasons for the use of teaching hours as a controlling device. First, the chairman of a department can better plan the assignment of his faculty colleagues by the hours required to teach in various types of instructional meetings. To plan this assignment in dollars involves the translation of hours into the almost fortuitous costs affected by the rank and salary of particular members. Departmental dollar costs are also affected by the changing pattern of leaves with salary, transfer to research, disability, and the assignment of personnel to interdepartmental or administrative activities. Teaching hours assigned to the courses or programs for which he is responsible provide a clear-cut administrative instrument for the chairman at the point of first responsibility.

The use of teaching hours to control costs is also helpful to the central administrator. Regardless of the current situation in departmental balance in rank, market influences on salary levels in particular fields, or fortuitous conditions with respect to leaves, he can thus ascertain, year by year, the relative intensity with which faculty time is used in the several departments employing a diverse mix of faculty ranks and instructional methods. He is in a stronger position to control expensive trends or new and costly experiments. He can demonstrate that new courses or new methods of instruction involve heavy future costs even though, for the time being, dollar costs are not greatly affected because of the use of younger and lower-salaried instructors.

Thus, control through teaching hours makes obvious the cost of additional courses, especially in an institution of relatively stable general enrollment. When courses are subdivided, the same number of students usually require more teaching hours. A very useful unit thus becomes the number of students taught per teaching hour. While some subjects, like exotic languages, may normally show a small unit value in students taught per teaching hour, courses in these subjects can easily become still more costly if not controlled. At the same time, counterbalancing economies in teaching costs measured in students taught per hour in departments of large enrollments, such as English and history, can be preserved only if specific measures of their use of hours are available year by year.

The use of the unit "students taught per teaching hour" in an institution using instructional methods of varying intensity in the application of faculty manpower may be illustrated. In a department such as English, the number taught, on an average, in a one-hour undergraduate lecture might be 100, in a one-hour class 15, and in a one-hour preceptorial conference 8; and for periodic tutorial conferences 5 students might be assigned to a professor for each teaching hour credited on his weekly schedule. The relatively high cost of small preceptorial meetings and individual tutorial conferences with students doing "independent" work becomes obvious. The economies gained through the large lecture groups in English and history are offset by the need to provide a far greater number of teaching hours for preceptorials and tutorial conferences in these popular departments. Should these departments seek permission to schedule three-hour seminars of fifteen students each—a form of meeting much desired by many faculty members and better undergraduates alike—the average teaching-hour cost must be put at five per hour, an extremely expensive figure.

To make teaching-hour costs real to the proponents of new and expensive instructional programs, it is possible for a dean to have ready each year an approximate average cost in dollars per teaching hour, using an average annual compensation and an average weekly teaching schedule for all ranks combined or for the senior ranks alone. This becomes a very impressive figure, especially if *net* teaching hours are used after the elimination of time assigned to administration, paid leaves, and other nonteaching functions. It is fair to add, also, an average overhead percentage for the cost of supporting staff and facilities directly related to the teaching function. Armed with such realistic estimates of cost, a dean can bring practical economics to bear on a discussion of new educational methods or coverage.

The measure of students taught per teaching hour is useful also in the year-by-year control of departmental manning, particularly that below the tenure level. Comparisons of averages for similar departments or for a period of years in the department concerned may be very persuasive in indicating loose administration of costly hours, the proliferation of small courses, or the excessive use of more expensive methods of instruction. The wide differences in departments must, however, be kept in mind. But a department teaching exotic languages needs tight control because it is already a high-cost operation, and a department of heavy enrollments like history may seek many new courses to satisfy its younger members. If faculty manning costs are not effectively measured and presented to those making curricular decisions, educational progress may end in institutional bankruptcy. The more expensive the operation, the tighter must be its controls.

While an educational administrator should not make the control of teaching costs his primary basis for judging changes in curriculum and instructional methods, he is the person in the university who must keep the need for sound economy in the use of manpower a significant factor in faculty-administration discussions. With adequate help to maintain and analyze data on manpower utilization, his influence upon the deliberations of faculty committees can be wholesome but not unduly restrictive on educational planning. A sense of economy improves any art and, applied to the use of precious talent in the art of developing further talent, it is peculiarly appropriate.

In addition to exercising oversight over the use of faculty manpower in instruction, the educational administrator has the responsibility of reviewing constantly the size and balance of the schools and departments in terms of the rank, age, and subject specialty of the faculty on appointment. In this activity he is faced with a host of variables, including the special interests and areas of strength of his institution, the accidents of turnover caused by resignation or disability, prospective retirements, the degree of promise of younger men, teaching requirements at various levels, the need for critical mass in a particular subject, and the vital need for one or more persons of leadership ability in each department. While it would be difficult, if not impossible, to present a common, effective pattern of manpower policy for diverse institutions, there are several general considerations which may be of use to those responsible for universitywide policy.

Experience has shown that the most critical factor in trends in instructional costs over time is the number of senior appointments made from year to year. While difficult to prove statistically, it is a good working hypothesis. It is particularly true in the liberal university in which enrollments are not changing rapidly. The reason is that new senior appointments usually involve new subfields in disciplines or, at least, new approaches to subfields which add high-level salary costs without a countervailing offset by the reduction of salary costs for the coverage of existing courses. It is also true that additional senior appointments usually involve additional junior staff in the subfield, specialized library resources, laboratory facilities, office space, secretarial assistance, and research support. It may also follow that additional fellowship funds will need to be provided to assure a flow of advanced students in the subfield. Altogether, the continuing concomitant costs of appointing a new senior professor may in time become from twice to three times the professor's annual salary. Such an increase would, of course, not occur if the new professor precisely replaced in the subfield covered a professor who has retired or resigned. But in the dynamic expansion and subdivision of knowledge today, this seldom happens. Most new appointments involve some degree of proliferation or shift in coverage. It is most difficult to close out older, declining fields as fast as new fields are added.

The older approaches to biology and geology continue to be the center of interest of older tenure members even after fields like molecular biology or geophysics must be manned. Older branches of engineering may need to be double-manned to recognize the need to teach applied science or sophisticated mathematical analysis. The center of interest in social science is shifting toward mathematical and behavioral approaches. It is far easier to recognize these changes in approaches than to shift the weight of competency and interest in a faculty composed in good part of members still years away from retirement.

For the educational administrator, the evolution of disciplines poses a continuing problem in dealing with schools and departments. The stronger a faculty, the more vigorous the demand to cover new and developing areas in almost every discipline. The faculty presses for differentiation within a field and for able and mature men to effectuate differentiation. The administrator, even though most anxious to see his institution stay at the forefront, must seek to control the rate of new appointments to allow some offset to take place through terminations. He must also encourage the use of younger, lower-salaried personnel in developing new fields and thus delay the full impact of change until turnover has occurred. Most of all, he must keep constantly before his chairmen the practical fact that choices must be made each year between disciplines and within disciplines if an institution is to remain solvent and pay adequate salaries to its existing faculty.

An effective device to implement wise budgeting of new appointments appears to be for the president to request early each fall a written justification of all proposals for new senior appointments, including promotions, for the following year and an estimate of needs thereafter. The president, in consultation with his chief educational administrators, then sets an overall university-wide limit on new appointments or senior promotions deemed possible, and assigns positions to the schools and departments with the greatest need. This procedure not only forces early planning, but allows a moving equilibrium of policy, year by year, assuring a balanced, integrated faculty.

A university faculty is like a tree in that all branches tend to grow smaller branches and twigs, yet some inner controls must assure the symmetry of the total organism. While the faculty, department by department, initiates the forces of growth, the administration, responsible for the educational and economic health of the institution, must determine what growth is justified and feasible in an integrated institution. This, it is believed, is no invasion of faculty prerogatives, but a means of assuring effective academic management on a cooperative basis in an institution facing sharply rising costs. To depend upon uncontrolled faculty initiative to determine new senior positions is to invite not only unbalanced growth but unbalanced budgets as well.

The chief educational administrator of a liberal university is called upon to judge men as well as to review manpower utilization and budgeting. While the evaluation of competency and promise in a discipline is most certainly the function of those in the discipline, the central administrator has not only the right but the obligation to judge a candidate for appointment as a person, so far as possible. A liberal university is concerned with the attributes of a candidate as a teacher of young people of talent, his interest in their development as persons as well as specialists, his willingness to share the responsibilities of departmental management, and his general understanding and acceptance of the obligations of faculty membership. To arrive at such judgments, it is a wise investment of funds to bring a candidate for tenure-level appointment to the campus for both a seminar and visit with his prospective colleagues and also a discussion of university aims and policies with the president or his chief educational officer, or both. Departments tend to emphasize the scholarly reputation of a candidate and have, at times, a weakness for "stamp collecting." The administrator is concerned with building an integrated human organization. A balance of tensions in this respect is wholesome, if mutual understanding exists.

It follows that if the educational administrator is concerned about the members of the faculty as individuals, he should be concerned with all the problems which individuals and their families face from time to time. This involves the administrator in *all* the financial and nonfinancial arrangements surrounding the employment relationship. The development of a sound and comprehensive system of "fringe benefits" will be discussed in a later chapter. It is sufficient to comment here that the planning and effectiveness of such a system are just as much the obligation of the educational administrator as of those on the business side of the university.

d. The Administration of Supporting Student Services

It has already been noted that the supporting academic services in universities have grown steadily in recent years in both size and relative importance. This is especially the case in the liberal university, which seeks to educate selected individuals for leadership in a wide range of careers. The increasing cost of liberal and professional education makes careful selection procedures and comprehensive financial-aid programs essential. Once admitted, the student needs continuing help in making wise choices of programs, in finding rewarding activities outside the curriculum, and in maintaining balance and tone in the demanding life on campus. There are several general principles which deserve consideration in determining the structure and relationships of the administrative staff dealing with the supporting services which provide the environment for a student's curricular education.

It is a sound premise to assume that everything which affects a student while he is enrolled in a liberal university should be looked upon as a part of his education. The student is a complex combination of intellectual, emotional, spiritual, and physical attributes and drives. He cannot be neatly dissected into parts. The central purpose for his being in the university is, however, the enhancement of his intellectual powers under the guidance of a faculty. Therefore, the faculty should assume the central and pervasive responsibility to assure that the various elements in the student's total experience are mutually reinforcing.

With the increasing degree of specialization, particularly in some areas in educational and clinical psychology, there has been a tendency for some faculties to hand over the major responsibility for the selection, placement, counseling, and disciplining of students to staff members more versed in psychological techniques than experienced in teaching. The assumed justification for such delegation is that the progress of modern science warrants the same division of labor in administration that it does in research. Unfortunately, the real reason may be avoidance by nonspecialists of a sticky business which involves time, energy, and tough decisions.

But the faculty must remain the integrating force in the total education of the young person. Specialists are needed to help in analysis and day-to-day services, but the essential purpose is to help the student, as a whole person, to gain from a complex learning experience. The faculty must make sure that, apart from the onset of physical or mental disability—when the physician relieves the teacher—the *total* educational program has balance and coherence.

In specific terms, the faculty through appropriate committees should help establish criteria for admission; help determine policies in student aid and employment; assure that counseling enhances independence and growing emotional and intellectual maturity; and make certain that discipline does not become sloppy and sentimental. For the healthy student, the university years should be a stretching, testing experience. He is not a patient, a client or, primarily, a subject for psychological research. The faculty, and not the specialist administrative staff, should establish the overall pattern of university experience.

This strong support of faculty responsibility is not intended to question the great contributions of professionally minded, nonfaculty administrators in dealing with the diverse problems of student life. With all the experience that universities have gained and all the research based on such experience, the effectiveness in implementing institutional policy in such supporting services still depends largely upon the dedication, wisdom, and constant insight of mature staff officers. Such officers may be as sensitive to the educational traditions and policies of their university as any faculty member, but to assure integration of total institutional policy they should be guided by and, in turn, help to guide an appropriate faculty committee. It is assumed that such a committee includes, preferably as chairman, a senior educational officer who represents the president and also serves as a leader and moderator in faculty-administrative cooperation.

To develop professionally minded persons for positions in the supporting staff related to student life will require more planning and effort in the years ahead than most universities have invested to date. It will require the organization of a nonfaculty "civil service" subject to policy determinations by the higher administration and the faculty but highly effective in its own professional sphere. With such a supporting staff, the central mission of the liberal education of the student should pervade the exercise of any particular skill or technique. It should be possible for staff members to move from one office to another as they gain experience and move ahead toward senior posts. While some specialties may not permit transfer across organizational structure, more flexibility is possible than is usually assumed. For example, the development of a first-class dean of students may include experience in admissions, student aid, counseling, placement, discipline, or even direction or coaching in specialized extracurricular activities. The common element is the liberal education of students and the understanding which can be gained on the campus of an institution that embodies a teaching approach in its administration as well as in its curricular endeavors.

As with young teachers, so with young administrators: the well-managed university should assume the functions of a teaching hospital. It should develop many more qualified officers than it can promote to senior posts. By so doing it increases the general supply of experienced supporting talent so greatly needed throughout higher education today. It also assures a flow of able, dedicated candidates to meet its own requirements in its junior staff. Further, it offsets an unfortunate tendency to resort to ready-made specialists fresh out of graduate schools of education who prefer to operate "by the book" as independent professionals rather than become a part of an integrated educational team with a common mission.

To make more concrete the concept of mutual reinforcement of supporting services and academic activities, a few examples may be helpful. It has been found that those in charge of student employment can be very helpful in making sure that work experience is truly educational and not merely a way of earning money. Students can be taught the arts of personnel management, accounting, and budgetary controls. They can learn the satisfactions of a job well done even though it consists of waiting on table in commons or running a student laundry. The problems of organizing food services, parking at games, or student furniture exchanges can be truly educational. With imagination, work opportunities can be developed in laboratories, libraries, and research programs which acquaint students with the main business of the university while providing them with money for work done.

Among the other teachers apart from the faculty itself are the coaches and instructors in intercollegiate and intramural athletics. They should be respected as such. In the liberal university, the most favorable results are gained if the entire staff is considered a special department of instruction and are on year-round, continuing appointment even though assignments shift from season to season. Policy with respect to intercollegiate athletics must be centered in the senior administration and faculty even though alumni and students participate in an advisory role. Respect for the interests of the individual student must be sustained by placing final authority concerning his health and physical welfare in the hands of the medical staff and that for his academic welfare in the hands of a faculty committee. Participation in intercollegiate contests, no matter how vital to a successful season, remains a means of education for the student and the institution alike.

The debate concerning the place of intercollegiate sports in higher education has continued for many decades. For a liberal university, neither the extreme of elimination nor that of national "big-time" competition seems desirable. In the development of emotional control, poise under stress, and courage, persistence, and enthusiasm under trying conditions, no other experience available to qualified students can do as much as a demanding schedule of intercollegiate contests. This can be as valuable a part of the education of the whole man as the solving of tough problems in mathematics. The good administrator and the good coach know that this is the main reason why intercollegiate athletics belong in a liberal university. A secondary reason is, of course, the enhancement of institutional loyalties and institutional personality in an area where interest and a sense of participation are readily aroused. It is when the secondary reason overrides the primary reason for intercollegiate sports that the trouble begins. In the administration of a liberal university, the structure, procedures, and traditions of control of intercollegiate athletics must be so safeguarded that the temptation to satisfy the more rabid alumni, the sports writers, and the viewing public is kept in constant check. The faculty and senior administration must exercise this control, no matter how thankless the job.

e. The Expanding Role of the University Library

The acceleration in the rate of accumulation of new knowledge and new concepts, particularly in the areas of science and social studies, has placed an additional and heavy responsibility upon the university library, a responsibility peculiar to our time. With the rapid development of new findings in science and new approaches to the problems of organized society, the university library has been called upon to bring together with speed and sensitivity vast streams of books, articles, and documents to form an effective instrument for further analysis and discovery. Thus the emphasis in library responsibility in our time has been increasingly broadened from conserving the learning of the past to include making the new knowledge of the present readily and systematically available.

The role of the library within the liberal university has also shifted in recent years from that of a passive contributor to being an active participant in the educational process itself. No longer satisfied with the stimulation of students' minds through transmitting old knowledge by means of lectures and texts, the faculties in our best liberal universities are encouraging their students to undertake independent study and research in wide-ranging fields. The library has become the place and instrument of education as never before. The student is called upon to seek knowledge and understanding for himself in the library or in the laboratory, and in a reinforcing combination of both. No longer is the library the resource of the teacher alone in preparing his lectures, but it has also become the workshop of the student in seeking the original sources of knowledge and the diverse interpretations of truth.

The inquiring student of today responds to the inquiring teacher-scholar who on his part uses the library as his daily workshop. As scholarship and research give tone to inspiring teaching, they also give deep satisfaction to the kind of teacher-scholar most needed in the great university. The able teacher-scholar today is attracted to an environment which provides not only keen students and stimulating colleagues, but also the means for his own self-development—a library of comprehensive coverage and effective organization sensitive to his needs. Thus the library has become an essential foundation and supporting mechanism in building a strong faculty in a time of great scarcity of the highest talent. While laboratories for scientists and engineers are physically more impressive than library stacks, the building and maintenance of excellent library resources and services in these fields in a time of rapid change have become highly desirable attributes in attracting and holding creative scholars. The university which starves its library soon finds its most promising teacher-scholars looking elsewhere for more adequate support.

The rapid enlargement of the functions of the library within the university caused by progress in scholarship and educational methods has found almost all such libraries unprepared in staff and resources. The accelerated flow of material to be acquired and organized is of itself overwhelming. But even more difficult to meet is the need for professionally trained staff, for specialists in dozens of disciplines and languages, and for the facilities and space to make material quickly and readily available. The older scholar in an older humanistic discipline gained over a long apprenticeship a command of the established bibliography of his subject. The younger scientist, now at the forefront of a fast-moving field, needs far more help in searching out and coordinating the myriad streams of published findings which may affect his research. The complexity of the periodical literature in science today is almost beyond the comprehension of the layman in its extreme specialization and its multiple interrelationships. Only the librarian of exceptional professional competence and understanding can provide adequate bibliographical support for those working in many frontiers of scientific discovery.

The problem of the university library in giving effective support to the scientist is paralleled by the difficulty of providing ready and comprehensive support to the social scientist. The primary sources of the student of public policy cover a vast range of official reports, newspaper accounts, journal articles, field studies, correspondence, and pamphlet material. Historical studies require the organization of the documentary files of influential leaders. The analysis of corporate, trade union, and institutional policies requires the accession and indexing of broad flows of ephemeral publications and more confidential material which must be sought out by specialists. The accelerating flow of texts and monographs in the social disciplines is the result of research carried on, in the first place, by university scholars and others using the primary sources channeled through the collecting and organizing mechanism of a dynamic library.

The concern of the student, the scholar, and the government with world affairs, as America has become an influential political and social force in every continent, has greatly expanded the demand upon the resources and services of the university library. The extension of coverage to an additional area of the world requires not only the accession and organization of current publications, but the building in of material on the history, literature, culture, anthropology, and linguistics of the region. A civilization as old as that of China, Korea, or Japan involves, for the librarian and the scholar, a degree of depth in historical materials and a breadth of diverse streams of cultural expressions comparable to those in Western civilization. The problems of acquiring and organizing such materials in a range of languages, old and new, are but typical of those thrust upon the library which serves a faculty with scores of area specialists, giving instruction to students who would understand the world today. The need of support is not alone that for liberal education and scholarship, but to assure that our government and our citizens can deal wisely with the peoples of other nations and cultures.

In these and many other ways, the university library has become the essential and central supporting mechanism of instruction and scholarship in a liberal university. The private library of the older scholar is still a useful and pleasure-affording adjunct to a life of study. But in most disciplines it has become a set of craftsman's tools in an age of complex industry. As the technology of industry has expanded with the coming of automation, computers, and systems analysis, so the methodology of the scholar, scientist, and research engineer must be reinforced by modern library resources, techniques, and organization. The laboratory scientist or the individual scholar, without the library, could still produce interesting and valuable findings and propositions, but he would be at sea without a compass in fitting his contribution into the accumulating fabric of truth. Without the library, each scholar would start anew and leave his addition to knowledge to the chance rediscovery of some later individual. With the library, comprehensive and well organized, he becomes an effective agent in the advancement of human understanding and the mastery of the problems of modern life.

To meet the rapidly growing needs of the library in a liberal university will require a greater concentration of attention and effort on the part of trustees, administration, and faculty than ever before. The library, in some ways, has been the Cinderella in university administration. It must now go to the ball. While the nub of the library's problem may appear to be largely financial, the greatest need is for sustained concern on the part of many others besides the dedicated but often lonely librarian and his staff of professional specialists. Although working in the middle of the campus, many librarians still feel that they are on the outer fringe of the community of teacher-scholars whom they serve.

There are understandable reasons for the relative isolation of the university library as an adjunct of instruction and scholarship from the mainstream of universitywide concerns and excitements. As with most facilitating services, whether provided by a restaurant waiter or by a gas company, efficiency is taken for granted and only shortcomings attract attention. A library gives no brilliant lectures and wins no thrilling games. Further, the notable accomplishments of a library are likely to fall into scattered, specific fields where only a few scholars are able to assess results. The scholar in history is little impressed by the collection in mathematics, but he is irked if some new research interest of his has not been anticipated years before. Much of the professional work of a library goes on behind the scenes and shows results only over time. New special collections of rare books may gain occasional public notice, but the growth of the main body of holdings seldom gets attention outside the librarian's annual report.

The case for a renaissance of support for the sharply expanding role of the library within the liberal university must come in the first instance from the faculty as both teachers and scholars. Such support will never, however, reach the decibels in tone of that for new faculty appointments or new areas of instruction. Since long periods of time and large sums of money are involved, the president and the senior educational officers of the university must convert a general faculty concern into major decisions of policy, funds, structures, and staff, and must convince the board of trustees of their wisdom. There is no more certain bulwark of quality for a great university than the possession of a distinguished library. Professors may come and go, but a library is on perpetual tenure.

The administrative facet of the strengthening and integration of the library in the total university organization involves the question of the status of professional librarians in relation to that of the teaching faculty who hold professorial rank. This is an issue which has become the subject of serious discussion in many universities. Where there is a university council or comparable body representing the various segments of the university in planning new developments or in assuring general balance and integration, the senior library staff should, of course, be adequately represented. Where it is the responsibility of those holding professorial rank to oversee the curriculum and methods of instruction and to take part in personnel procedures, the introduction of library staff as voting members of the faculty, as so defined, involves an inconsistency between the area of normal functional experience and the area of responsible decision.

It is true that librarians are more directly concerned with day-by-day academic pursuits than any other supporting, professional group in the university. The work of those engaged in the search for scholarly materials parallels much of the activity of scholars. But it remains important to distinguish the faculty in its managerial function from the faculty as an inclusive academic community. The professional librarians should hold highly respected status as a member of the academic community, with such hierarchical ranking as seems appropriate, but his means of influencing policy and progress in his area of concern should be other than participating in the myriad determinations which are involved in the administration of curriculum, instruction, teaching schedules, admissions, standing, student discipline, research programs, and faculty appointments and advancements. These are the responsibility of those who hold professorial rank as teacher-scholars, discipline by discipline, as well as in the general faculty as a managerial body. While there are bound to be overtones of status in the assignment of any traditional titles, the nub of the question is function and the assignment of responsibility related to function.

The university librarian should be a senior academic officer of the university and his chief assistants may be given, as a means of recognition of their vital contribution, an appropriate equivalent rank. But to make all professional librarians voting members of the faculty and determiners of educational policy confuses both organization and function. The position of the library as such should be recognized by more substantial means. The status of the librarians, as individuals, can be better enhanced by improved salaries, by greater professional opportunities, such as paid leaves for study, and by the more positive recognition and support by the teaching faculty in the essential functions they perform.

The relations between the teaching faculty and the library

staff can be strengthened in many ways as the need for more comprehensive and effective library support is recognized. Not only should the general faculty committee on the library be a constant channel of intercommunication, but it should also be a positive means of indicating the interest of the faculty in adequate university support for the needs of the library. Department by department, the specific needs of each discipline should be adequately represented by members assigned to this responsibility. No longer can the library be the sole interest of some self-appointed professor of bookish tastes; it should be the common responsibility of the department in assuring the sustained support of its instruction and scholarship in the years ahead. Particularly in rapidly moving fields in science, social science, and engineering, faculty members should be close advisers to librarians specializing in the procedures necessary to assure the ready availability of flows of current materials. In sum, in the liberal university of the future, the library must become an integral and dynamic element in instruction and scholarship and no longer a separate adjunct patiently performing a routine service on an inadequate budget.

f. The Administration of Academic Budgets

It is not within the scope of the present analysis of the problems of the liberal university to enter upon a general discussion of the complex area of financial and business administration. Not only are there others whose experience qualifies them far better to discuss university finances, but it is probable that most of the problems concern all types of universities regardless of the educational philosophy of the institution. There are, of course, differences in financial practices between public and private universities, but these are more related to laws than to purpose. The brief discussion which follows is intended to cover certain considerations related to finances in which the educational philosophy of the liberal university may affect the financial administration of the institution.

Because of its emphasis upon a broader and more fundamental education of the individual student at all levels, even in graduate programs, and, at the same time, upon a faculty engaged in fundamental rather than applied scholarship and research, the liberal university has difficulty demonstrating a "value return on investment." This does not relieve the academic administrator from thorough study of the probable cost and the probable contribution of every new expenditure; it does mean that the expected return on most outlays will need to be judged in qualitative rather than quantitative terms in furthering the university's goals and services. For example, should the coverage of solid-state physics be expanded as an alternative to filling a critical vacancy in the classics? The probable cost of each alternative may be carefully estimated as $20,000 a year, but the expected returns must be evaluated in terms of the university's commitment to both the advancement of science and the preservation of our cultural heritage as well as to liberal education. Unlike the great service university, the liberal university cannot give critical significance to the number of students who will enroll in a particular field, or the classics would have long since withered. Yet it may seriously weaken its position in science if it waits too long before entering a rapidly developing area of discovery. The decision is a difficult one and must be considered in terms of the mission of a particular university and not of enrollments alone. Even if prospective enrollments were used as a critical test, there would remain the question of whether the world needed ten men educated in physics more than it needed five young scholars educated in the classics.

Further, many decisions on alternative investments involve factors of intensity and quality in education. The elimination of a hundred hours of preceptorial instruction might, let us say, offset the net instructional cost of admitting twenty-five more students per class. Would the additional number educated counterbalance the loss in the quality of educational service rendered the then larger undergraduate body? It is sufficient to premise that the value of the "output" must be estimated in *educational* terms even though the cost of the "input" is carefully measured in dollars.

The consequence of these conditions in the liberal university is that its budget officer in financial administration must rely far more heavily upon the judgment of his senior academic associates in the administration than upon precise financial data. While he must constantly advise the president and the chief educational officers of the size of the cloth of available funds, the pattern, department by department, must be determined by complex educational considerations. The budget officer can watch and report trends in faculty costs. He can be especially effective in reviewing supporting expenditures for nonacademic staff, for laboratory facilities and research operations, and for space, supplies, and services. But it is in the nature of the essential function of a liberal university that relative costs, area by area, do not assure readily comparable gains when the product is, not soap, but men of talent and contributions to insight and knowledge for generations to come.

A practical way of meeting the dilemma of keeping academic expenditures within the limits set by available funds, year by year, is to divide out the segments of budgetary control according to the focus of responsibility in planning. The most critical segment is that of new senior appointments or promotions to cover new areas of instruction and research. The determination here is one for the president and his senior academic officers to make, once the general estimate of available funds is provided by the financial officer. It can be best resolved in terms of the senior positions to be authorized, as discussed earlier. New senior positions, of course, must be balanced against known and probable turnover through retirements and other terminations. In a liberal university, the coverage of areas is so much more influential than enrollments in its long-run effect that the decision on the precise positions to be authorized or continued is a critical consideration and one to be made at the highest academic level.

A second segment which can be divided out is that of expenditures for junior personnel, department by department, as affected by enrollments. In those universities with but gradual growth, a projection from past experience, with a modest reserve for sudden shifts, can be used by the educational officer in his discussions with his financial counterpart. Teaching requirements at this level tend to follow established norms unless sharp changes in methods occur. Also, shifts are likely to be mutually offsetting and to involve lower-than-average salary costs in terms of students taught.

A third segment is that covering changes in salary level through merit increases or changes in scale at all academic ranks. The relative need for such increases or changes in raising the level of faculty salaries to meet outside competition is for the chief academic officers to determine by assessment of counteroffers, recruiting experience, and available surveys. The availability of funds and the necessary allocations for increases in the salaries of persons outside the faculty are the concern of the financial and business administration.

There remains the fourth general segment, the control of expenditures for the supporting staff, equipment, space, facilities, supplies, and services related to instruction and research but of a nature to be closely interrelated with the business operations of the university. This appears to be primarily the province of the financial and business administration, but with the advice of the senior academic officers to reflect changing needs in particular areas.

The approach outlined suggests the increasingly close cooperation between the academic and financial officers which is necessary if the liberal university is to meet the financial stringencies of the future. The goal of the future is effective *academic* management in which planning is done by senior officers who, regardless of title, have a keen sense of both educational needs and economic feasibility. That university is blessed which has educators who understand costs and financial officers who can interpret mission. The day is past when the treasurer of a liberal university can act like a banker or the manager of an investment trust concerned only with the balance sheet.

A means of coordinating the academic and financial aspects of university operation at a point close to daily operations is the appointment, as earlier suggested, of qualified administrative assistants to departmental chairmen and deans of schools. Such administrative assistants can relieve the chairmen or deans of the management of the supporting staff and services and, at the same time, can help prepare and implement budgets. They can also assist in assessing needs for junior teaching personnel, in handling research contracts, and in assuring the best use of space and equipment. In so doing, working closely with a chairman or dean, they help bring to focus at the first-line level the concept of *academic* management so needed in universities today. As a part of the academic civil service, previously discussed, such departmental administrative assistants are well worth the investment in their salaries and development.

5

THE
TRUSTEES

The primary function of the board of trustees in American higher education is to determine and sustain the purpose of the institution. This function grew out of the formation of colleges to provide ministers and other professional leaders in the colonies and the young nation. In the private liberal college and university, this traditional concern of the board with education for leadership still persists despite the secularization of control and the broadening of the scope of instruction and scholarship. In the state universities, as well as other public institutions, a board is intended to sustain the purpose of the institution to enhance, by broadening the opportunities for higher education, the welfare and enlightenment of the community which supports the institution through taxes. The purposes of the two types of institutions increasingly overlap. However, the fact that the boards of private, liberal institutions are mainly self-perpetuating emphasizes the importance of tradition and institutional personality rather than general public opinion in the interpretation of purpose by the boards of liberal institutions.

The secondary but more visible function of the board of trustees of a university is to make sure that funds and structures are available to sustain the established purpose of the institution. A board, it may be said, is concerned first with ends, then with means, but only indirectly with method. It is obvious that the legal power to control means permits invasion of the area of methods, but restraint in this respect has become a firm tradition with most boards, strengthened by sensitivity on the part of both the board itself and the faculty. The sustaining of purpose as contrasted to involvement in method also requires restraint. It is a function served more by the communication of assumptions than by overt direction. Only on rare occasions does a board need to exercise its legal authority to restrict or direct a change in the purposes of an institution.

The most effective way in which a board of trustees makes sure that the established purposes of the institution are sustained is by the appointment of a president who embodies those purposes. As has been discussed, the purposes and values of a liberal university involve too many intangible factors to be adequately expressed in resolutions or rules. Once the board, after soul-searching deliberation, selects a president, it must rely upon him in the largest measure possible to be their channel in communicating purpose to those who make up the institution.

As in most situations where complex ideas and values are communicated, the interchange between a board and a president must involve a continuing program of discussions, both formal and informal. These discussions must, to be useful, relate to events, developments, plans, and policies. Those related to purposes may take place largely in the sessions of relevant trustee committees where time permits thorough review. Such committees may include, among others, one concerned with curriculum, instruction, and faculty appointments, and another dealing with admissions, student life, health, athletics, and other extracurricular activities.

A good part of the meetings of such committees should include reports by the president and his senior academic officers, that is, the academic administration. The committee of the board gives occasion for a periodic review of progress and for the clear presentation of plans. It is through the questions and comments of the board members related to specific developments or plans that two-way communication occurs. By full disclosure of concerns and contemplated measures, well in advance of final decision, the board through discussion has an opportunity to influence policy without assuming administrative responsibility. It is an old comment that, in a successful continuing relationship between a board and an administration, the more an administration tells a board, the less the board tells the administration what to do. This is particularly important on the academic side of the board-administration axis, since here the administration is itself dealing with a widely diverse faculty, as well as a complex process, in which response is more vital to success than authoritative direction.

The presence of senior academic officers in meetings with committees of the board should in no way obscure the essential fact that the board's proper and most effective channel of communication in terms of institutional purpose is the president. The other officers are present to provide information and to discuss plans in detail. It is the part of wisdom for them to introduce no significant evidence and no personal recommendations which have not previously been discussed with the president. The board members deserve the integrated judgment of the administration, through the president, and not merely the separate opinions of officers of limited jurisdiction. A second device to clarify board-administrative relationships is for the president to assume full responsibility for presenting or discussing academic matters at meetings of the *full* board. It can be assumed that the discussions in the committees, with other academic officers present, have covered the issues upon which more specialized information or experience is needed.

The maintenance of the general tone of trustee-administration relations here outlined is of great importance in dealing with faculty appointments and specific curricular programs. In these areas, the faculty has, after full deliberation, made its recommendations. The president and his senior officers have participated in the deliberations and concurred in the recommendations. While the board reserves the legal power to appoint professors and approve degrees, it should exercise sustained restraint in intervening in a particular academic decision of this nature. The board has the right to have as complete information on proposed appointments or programs as it desires, but such decisions are essentially steps in the implementation of policy. In an institution where mutual respect exists, such decisions should not become issues of policy in themselves.

An exception to the degree of delegation here suggested might occur when a new school or department of instruction is proposed which requires a considerable financial investment. The board's involvement in this case may concern a question of means as well as that of the broad purposes of the institution. In such a matter, the views of the faculty must be balanced by the judgment of those having a long-run interest in the traditions and financial health of the university. Again the president must assume the key role in resolving the issues of means, methods, and ends after full consultation with the proper committees of the board.

With respect to the provision of means rather than the sustaining of purpose, the relations between the board of trustees and the president and his chief financial and business officers are much more direct, positive, and definite. The board must review financial reports, approve budgets, and determine plans for construction. It is legally responsible for the safeguarding of funds and property. While administrative *operations* are the function of full-time institutional officers, the judgment of trustees reflects their special competency and long-run obligations in assuring the solvency of the enterprise. It is still important that a board express a judgment on policy as a *group*, whether in a committee or in the full board, rather than intervene as individuals in the administration. The financing of an educational institution involves special considerations which require the development of insights not readily transferred from most other forms of enterprise. Such insights are gained over time through discussions between board members and the professional administrators.

It is in its continuing recognition of the nature and purposes of *liberal* education that the board of an older liberal university may serve a function somewhat different from its counterpart in a great state multiversity. The concept and contributions of liberal education are not so universally understood that they can be taken for granted. The surest way for most people to come to an understanding of liberal education is to undergo the process and then enjoy its benefits in a successful career. This becomes an even more effective process if a board member can enhance his understanding by serving the institution he knows best—his alma mater. The presence of many alumni on the boards of older liberal institutions is not merely a pleasant, "school-tie" custom, but an important and conscious policy in preserving a particular kind of institution in a changing world. The member of the governing board of a state university may be selected to represent the various interests in a community in terms of *current* needs for a wide range of educational services. The member of the governing board of a liberal university, while concerned with education for leadership in the community at large, is also concerned with sustaining and enhancing a long-tested approach in developing that leadership. He may be biased by an "autobiographical" philosophy of education but, it is hoped, he is biased in the right direction.

This suggests that board members of liberal institutions should be given full opportunity to refresh and enlarge their understanding of the educational process in terms of today's conditions. Rotating service on a committee which has general oversight over the educational policies of the university and which, as has been suggested, has frequent opportunities to meet with academic officers and a faculty committee on conference, has proved to be one valuable means of such continuing education. This experience permits the board member to speak with more knowledge and conviction when questioned concerning the higher costs or relatively smaller enrollments which a liberal approach to higher education usually involves.

But the challenges to liberal higher education are not limited to those who question relative costs and output. Within the liberal university itself, the inclination of able, specialized scholars to produce brilliant young specialists in their own image is strong. It has been said that every well-knit professional body is a conspiracy against the laity. A faculty can gradually shift the purpose of a liberal university to the preparation of specialists at the expense of the balancing flow of well-educated generalists that are needed in the leadership of a democratic society. A subtle but significant function of the board of trustees of a liberal university is to reflect its concern for a quality of education in its institution, whether undergraduate or graduate, which fits men for the broader responsibilities of leadership in their careers and in the world.

The means of securing alumni representation on boards of trustees vary. In some private institutions it is traditional to favor alumni for life or term trustees, nominated and elected by the board itself. A tested procedure is to provide for the election of a fixed number of additional "alumni" trustees by the total alumni body or by regions on rotation. Some "alumni" trustees may prove to be such valuable additions to the board during their term in office that continuance by election by the board itself may prove desirable. It is probably advisable to blend the various procedures of choosing new members, since not all candidates of high qualification are well known, and a balance of professional and business experience of various kinds is highly desirable.

It is sometimes proposed that relations between the board of trustees and the faculty of a university would be improved if a small number of the faculty were elected to the board. There appears to be little favorable experience to justify this arrangement. It departs from the sound principle that the president should be the channel for communicating the recommendations of the faculty as a whole to the board and that he is in the best position to do so with full knowledge and impartiality. Further, the better way of assuring communication in the area of most concern to the faculty—educational policy—is through the joint discussions of an appropriate committee of the board and a conference committee elected by the faculty itself. Because such discussions can be informal and unofficial, they are more likely to be informative than are the brief remarks which a "faculty" board member can make in a meeting covering a wide range of other subjects.

If the point of view of a professional educator is to be most useful in the discussions of a board of trustees, it appears preferable that the educator be selected from outside the institution and have the same level of professional standing in his field as the lawyers, doctors, bankers, and industrial executives chosen for membership. Even then, the outside educator must remember that with respect to the academic program of the university he, as a board member, is concerned with broad issues of policy and not with detailed administration. The president can, of course, seek his professional advice as he would that of a lawyer or banker on the board, but an outside educator should be most cautious to avoid the role of an omniscient expert. It is most disconcerting to have on the board a "back-seat driver" who feels that he can run the institution better than the president can.

In a time of rapid change in the conditions and challenges faced by the university, there are those who argue that the average age of trustees in many institutions is too high to expect them to understand or approve the adjustments which an institution should make to meet these new conditions. To hold down average age and to avoid the sentimental fondness for earlier days which old age accentuates, there is strong reason for a strict rule for transfer of members to *emeritus,* nonvoting status at some age, probably seventy. Further, additions to a board should be concentrated in the younger ages, more in line with the younger ages of newly appointed professors and administrators in today's world.

Yet the function of a board of trustees in a liberal university suggests the compatibility of an older *average* age than that of a tenure faculty. While professors in many areas are concerned with the newly discovered frontiers of knowledge, the trustees must conserve the traditions, the personality, and the purposes of the institution. Again it is the difference between methods and ends. The latter change but slowly and can be better understood in a perspective gained by long experience. Neither the rapidity of change nor the increasing precociousness of younger scholars necessarily justifies an alteration in the long-established mission of the institution.

Among the traditions which a board must maintain are those of the academic freedom of the *institution* and the academic freedom of the *individual teacher* within the institution. That these two freedoms are distinct but mutually reinforcing is not widely understood. A board of trustees must serve as a buffer between an academic community, both as a corporate body and with respect to its individual members, and the large number of respectable people who do not understand that the vital purpose of academic freedom is to advance the discovery of truth. It must also stand fast when, in their enthusiasm in presenting their particular view of truth, members of the faculty or student body within the institution interfere with the exercise of freedom on the part of other members or students, or of the institution itself.

But the board of trustees of a liberal university must be more than a buffer in preserving a tradition of freedom. It must help to sustain the climate in which freedom truly contributes to human welfare, a climate which assumes such basic attributes as integrity, responsibility, and a concern for excellence. This it demonstrates corporately in its dealings with all concerned, year after year. These qualities are also reflected in the character of the individual members of the board. It is for this reason that, in the selection of members of a board, the personal attributes and standards of the candidate must be consistent with those which the institution upholds in its faculty and students.

To perform its functions effectively in sustaining means and total mission in the life of the university, a board of trustees must gain for itself a sense of ongoing personality of its own. It cannot become merely a visiting committee whose principal function is to hear reports and pass on budgets. If meetings of the board are too infrequent, it is difficult to develop a sense of involvement and group consciousness based upon the free discussion of diverse opinion. If, however, meetings occur too often, there is a temptation for the board to intervene in administration.

Various mechanisms have been developed to assure an effective compromise between under- and over-participation of boards in the affairs of a university. These include an executive committee with relatively frequent meetings and other committees with meetings spaced according to function, either between the meetings of the full board or just prior to them. The chairman of the executive committee can become a particularly valuable channel of communication between the president and the board, as well as a wise adviser to the president in times of urgent need. Since conditions of location, size of board, and type of institution vary widely, there appears to be no single ideal schedule. But the need for a sense of involvement based on full and frank communication, free discussion, and a corporate, self-conscious responsibility is made clearly evident by the unfortunate developments in some long-established institutions in recent years. When troubles come, it is a source of strength to have a well-informed, cohesive, and responsible board.

It was suggested earlier that it is helpful in a liberal university for the president to serve as chairman of the board of trustees. In that position, it is believed, he is better able to plan and guide the meetings of the board to assure full communication and discussion of all matters with which the board should be concerned and, at the same time, to avoid ill-advised excursions into the administrative implementation of policy. An effective president, like the effective chairman of a faculty committee, can create a framework for a fruitful discussion of policy which enhances wisdom at the same time that it assures responsible participation. Perhaps in this respect, as well as in dealings with a faculty, the experience which a president may have had as a teacher pays valuable dividends.

There has been a growing belief on the part of many observers of higher education in America that boards of trustees are coming to have less influence upon their institutions than in the past. The growing complexity of university administration has required the development of a core group of professional executives. Outstanding professors have strong ties to their discipline and are less dependent upon a particular institution for either employment or research support. More recently, students have begun to demand a greater share in the determination of policies affecting their way of life. There is much reason to expect a gradual readjustment in the relative degrees of influence which the various participants in a long-evolving and sensitive kind of human institution exercise.

But the broad functions of a board of trustees which have been analyzed are more important than ever in preserving the character and purposes of a liberal university. The university and the administration, faculty, and students of the university need a board more than is often realized. In a time of rapid change, acute problems, and sharp differences in interests, most institutions need the longer perspective which a board can provide. Making this longer perspective significant will require a greater degree of knowledge, understanding, and responsible participation in its proper areas of policy than many boards have sought. Most board members, as laymen, are hesitant in seeking the knowledge which would make their views relevant. A university administration and faculty which want a strong and wise board in times of change and consequent trouble must make that board strong and wise by years of mutually rewarding interaction with respect to the mission of the institution. As has been emphasized repeatedly, the president has the key role in assuring such interaction.

6

THE
STUDENT

It is, fortunately, not necessary or useful in an analysis of academic administration to analyze all the causes of unrest among young people in America and throughout the world today. It would be easy to repeat the usual diagnoses which have been suggested, including the Vietnam War, the draft, increasing affluence, naïve idealism, paternal permissiveness, and impatience with governments in providing solutions to the pressing problems of racial relations, poverty, and education. Young people enrolled in a university are an articulate, relatively intelligent, and highly visible segment of their generation. They are influenced by all the conditions which lead to uncertainty, frustration, and impatience with a world not of their making. The university is an immediate symbol of authority, and, along with other established institutions, it must bear its share of criticism. The intent of the following discussion is to analyze briefly the specific conditions within the control of the university which may, given the general unrest of young people of college age, have accentuated *student* unrest. Anyone who has dealt with students over many years need not be warned that any generalizations concerning them are highly tentative.

The relative affluence of the United States in recent years compared to a half-century ago has both accelerated and extended the process of formal education for an increasing proportion of our young people. Improved educational methods and facilities have sped up the progress of many, so that subject matter previously covered in the early years of college has been moved down to the high schools. At the same time, the economic and social advantages of a college education have now been recognized as associated even more fully with professional, postgraduate education, and many young people who a generation ago would have been earning a living in industry are now being supported in advanced instruction on into their mid-twenties.

There is much reason to believe that extending the period of formal education at the expense of a shift to effective, self-supporting accomplishment is not always compatible within the individual with the deep-set requirements for personal adjustment to increasing maturity. There has always been a small segment of any generation in a civilized society that has found a life of thoughtful inquiry a continuing source of satisfaction. Others have felt powerfully driven to acquire learning to become the clergy, the lawyers, and the doctors of the community. But today, with a far larger proportion of young people in our universities, there are many without such compelling drives who are continuing in an environment set up for thoughtful inquiry or intensive, professional training, when they have reached a stage in life when greater satisfactions could be gained by earning their living supporting others rather than being supported. Motivation, not intelligence, is the critical factor. For these young people, self-rationalization and the too-ready acceptance of the high value placed by society upon advanced learning in an age of science will not submerge a persistent want for the kind of accomplishment which generations of their ancestors have found necessary for happiness.

The unrecognized conspiracy to delay the shift from learning to earning has other participants than the student who finds the campus a pleasant refuge from the world. Parents who have won affluence through early and arduous effort are peculiarly disposed to shield their children from that valuable and maturing experience. Universities, on their part, need graduate students to teach a rising flood of undergraduates. A democratic government must provide the means of satisfying an electorate convinced that higher education is a right of all and not a privilege, so long as minimum requirements are met.

In a society in which external objects and experiences, from color-TV sets, new cars, swimming pools, speedboats, and a multitude of gadgets to a trip to Miami or Paris, have come to be the solace for internal unrest, it is not too hard to understand why young people not deeply involved in continuing education do not diagnose the cause of their frustration. Yet education, properly defined, is not a "purchase" paid for by someone else. It is a personal investment of a part of oneself. Unless one makes adequate investment, no matter how intelligent one may be, the psychic returns may be meager. If neither a love of inquiry nor a compelling ambition to gain professional competency is present, it is hard to make that investment. The result for those caught in this situation is a sense of frustration and, often, an attempt to place the blame on others rather than oneself: on the dullness or irrelevancy of courses, the indifference of teachers, the aloofness of administrators, or the arbitrary and unenlightened policies of all those in authority. The dropout from college or graduate school who gets a job in industry is on the way to providing his own cure for frustration. The student who persists in an academic environment for which he is poorly adjusted becomes the candidate for the emotional sprees which, no matter what their apparent objective, feed upon the frustrations of their participants. Intelligence may provide plausible excuses for their actions, but the driving force is emotional.

It would be unfair to today's students to explain away all unrest on campuses as due to a greatly increasing proportion of those who do not find self-fulfillment in the demanding experience of higher education. Rather than moving to meet the need of the student for a better understanding of his or her role in the educational process, increasing enrollments and an increasing emphasis upon professional attainment on the part of faculty members have broadened the gap between the student and the mature teacher. Large lectures, quiz sections led by graduate students, and counseling specialists trained in psychology are poor substitutes for the person-to-person interaction of an experienced and enthusiastic teacher of a discipline and a student whose motivation for learning needs stimulation. That education is more than a pedestrian intellectual effort in accumulating *knowledge* becomes evident when the emotional involvement of the student is minimal. Instead of better teaching to involve the broader flows of less avid scholars, limitations on qualified manpower and on funds have required the resort to "mass-production" methods.

The condition of student dissatisfaction is not, however, limited to universities of large and rising enrollments. A faculty member deeply engaged in his own research or in consulting off campus can be as distant from the individual student in a prestigious institution of limited enrollment as a lecturer in an auditorium seating thousands. Even the graduate student attending a distinguished university has cause for complaint if interaction with his professors is largely limited to formal dispensations of prepared discourses without an opportunity for free discussion. Heavy chores of handling quiz sections and reading examinations have come to be the lot of many graduate student apprentices in academia in the same way that apprentices in older times swept out the shop and did the duller, routine tasks. An advantage of the apprentices to a manual craft was that there were usually fewer of them.

But there may be a deeper, more subtle cause for dissatisfaction on the part of the student in higher education today. Regardless of his degree of motivation as a scholar in the terms which a professor appreciates, the young person in his more thoughtful moments is seeking satisfying answers to big questions which will affect *his* life in a time of national and international tensions. His ideas and ideals are not likely to fit into some precisely organized course in which the mature specialist has divided out a neatly manageable analysis. The great growth of specialization, the atomization of curriculums, and the development of the multiversity itself, while closely reflecting the interest of the professor-scholar and the apparent needs of large-scale bureaucratic administration, brings the student face to face with a vast and complex educational mechanism, when what he may need most is a few dedicated teachers interested in the questions which deeply concern him. The multiversity may be the source of rich streams of new knowledge, but it faces serious handicaps in satisfying the quest of young people today for an understandable and workable philosophy of life in a time of rapid social change. Such quests are better pursued where mature teachers in a wide range of subjects are ready to match their time and interest in close interaction with individual students considered as thinking, feeling persons and not as rows of note-takers. The premise that a multiversity should not be concerned with a student's philosophy of life may be at the bottom of much of today's unrest. At a time when fundamental values are involved in many current issues, neutrality and "scientific" objectivity offer little help.

Even if the motivation of the individual student and the character of the educational process were all that one could desire, there are reasons to believe that the lack of adequate channels of communication between the academic establishment and the community of students in the American university would be a cause for concern. In a type of human organization in which response is far more influential than command, upward communication is a vital factor in a sound evolution of policy. Further, the desire for participation in determining the arrangements within which one works and lives grows more in parallel to one's intellectual sophistication than to one's hard-won practical judgment. The present-day student wants and should have improved channels of communication up through the several levels of institutional organization. This should result in a more sensitive and effective response in the evolution of educational policy and at the same time should resolve tensions into a more wholesome climate of mutual understanding. The precise point at which communication shifts subtly into an authoritative voice in the determination of policy is the problem which must concern the academic administrator.

In the general study of human organizations it is an axiom that authority and responsibility must be precisely coordinate at any level or in any segment of organization if confusion, friction, and disintegration are to be avoided. Further, it is assumed in effective organization that authority and responsibility are based upon an understanding of the consequences of one's decisions upon the segment involved and consequently upon the total organization. In an industrial corporation, built upon a system of line authority, these principles appear to be clear-cut and practical. But in a university, the sharing of authority and responsibility is already so complex that the apparently simple problem of determining the precise character and degree of participation of the student community in authoritative decisions becomes a difficult one.

It has been through the evolution of the faculty-administrative committee that the university has found a way of combining a mechanism for focusing the channels of communication with the same body which initiates or considers policy. Under arrangements long found successful, the committee, through its administrator-chairman, is able to review policy, once approved, as it is implemented in administration. The great advantage of the committee mechanism is that it affords the opportunity to bring together *both* diverse disciplines and diverse segments of the university community. Therefore a committee which joins faculty and administration can also join faculty, administration, and students in a carefully structured relationship.

The most successful arrangements for bringing students into communication with and influence upon university policy in its more critical areas of student relationships appear to be through such multiconstituent committees. This by no means replaces committees or councils of students alone in the administration of their campus activities, in their consideration of policies and programs *ex parte*, or in the organized self-discipline involved in an honor system or a fraternity. Nor does it imply that students need participate in departmental meetings or in an advisory committee on faculty appointments and salaries. But certain areas of interaction between faculty, administration, and the student body appear to be appropriate for the use of multiconstituent committees which include student representation.

In the area of student discipline, for example, a tested arrangement is to include a minority representation of students, perhaps three, in a committee including, perhaps, six faculty members and a dean of students as chairman. In the development of policy and regulations, the point of view of students is brought to bear at the point of decision, but it is not necessarily compelling. On the other hand, it can be established that decisions involving the dismissal or longtime suspension of individual students must be unanimous and later confirmed by the faculty as a whole. Thus there must be a unanimous consensus of both faculty and student representatives to recommend a drastic action in an individual case without impairment of the faculty's authority and responsibility over discipline as a whole.

Experience suggests that such arrangements as outlined find that students are more ready to dismiss a fellow student for "unsportsmanlike conduct," such as stealing or other dishonesty, than faculty members more sophisticated in clinical psychology. On the other hand, students brought up in a more permissive age are likely to press for more liberal and less prescriptive parietal rules affecting their social life. The interplay of older and younger points of view is constructive. The important attribute of the committee approach is that there can be frank and intelligent discussion within a group charged with responsibility, rather than *ex parte* polemics and a sharpening of dissension.

In the planning of an undergraduate curriculum, there has been the assumption on the part of the faculty for many years that a student's freedom to choose what he wanted counterbalanced the faculty's right to offer what it thought best. This implied bargain might have gone unchallenged if more faculty members had retained a deep and responsible interest in undergraduate instruction as opposed to interest in graduate instruction and research. Further, for many undergraduates today, the freedom to elect one's department and courses is limited by requirements, real or assumed, for entrance into professional graduate programs. The time has come to add a limited number of student representatives to the general faculty committee on undergraduate curriculum. Again a channel of communication would be formalized without a dissipation of faculty responsibility. The final authority for the approval of courses would continue in the faculty, but the committee initiating recommendations for change might be more sensitive to student response and a little less so to the desires of ambitious specialists.

In these and other committees dealing with areas of joint concern, it is easier to arrange an improved interface between students and faculty than it is to make sure that the students on the committees have effective and responsible communication with their fellow students. This is a common problem in all representative government. In the university, the problem exists in assuring communication between chairmen and their departments, between committee members and the faculty generally, and also between student representatives and the general student body. All that can be suggested is that all administrators should continuously encourage free and widespread communication downward and outward to reduce the number of querulous complaints: "Nobody asked me what I thought about it." It is also true that the frustrated type of student who finds the excitement of protest against authority and all accepted forms of behavior a psychic catharsis will not be fully satisfied. It is the hard-learned experience of an older academic administrator that some students (and even some professors) would be unhappy if they had nothing about which to be unhappy.

While important in terms of universitywide relations and general educational policy, representation of students on a central committee on the undergraduate course of study, to be truly effective, needs a supporting structure of improved communication between students and faculty within each department. The simplest form of such communication is the request by an instructor for comments, written or oral, by the students in a course at the end of the term. A more formal procedure is a discussion session at the end of each academic year, to which the chairman of a department invites a small committee of departmental students. In such a session, the various features of courses, including lectures, group meetings, readings, papers, and examinations, can be considered in a comparative evaluation without the embarrassment of emphasizing the personal characteristics of individual instructors. To the astute chairman, the overtones of student opinion of the teacher come through without involving the students in a sense of unfairness to a dedicated but less effective instructor. Rather, in the climate of discussion it can be established that both courses and methods of instruction throughout the department can be improved if all possible suggestions are available to those responsible for the department as a whole. The advantage of group discussion is that students usually differ in their opinions, and a chairman can often clarify purposes, relationships, and limiting conditions which influence the planning of any instructional program.

A still more elaborate system of communication, which seems to have an enticing appeal in an era of questionnaires and computers, is the universitywide poll of course ratings compiled in arithmetic grades. The difficulty with such polls is that student-operated polls are likely to be of questionable validity because of uneven coverage or seriousness of response, whereas university-operated polls become expensive. Even the best of polls in terms of planning, coverage, and analysis remain a one-way process of communication, and evaluations are made without the means for clarifying terms and encouraging careful consideration which interviews can provide. While near-unanimous ratings at either extreme may afford clear evidence, such evidence is usually readily attainable through less elaborate procedures. Polls are more useful if the various elements of each course are evaluated separately, but this adds to the problem of gaining full response and to the expense of compilation. The qualitative comments attached to returns are often more helpful than the grades indicated.

In summary, it appears clear that the most constructive method of communication between the faculty and the student in respect to the character and quality of the educational program is thc same as the best means of education itself—face-to-face, inter-active discussion. Modern techniques of estimating mass response have the appeal of "science," but they are likely to divert to statistical measurement effort which might be better spent on making more sensitive and responsive the less "objective" processes of communication between the student and the teacher and between the student body and those responsible for the total educational program.

It has been suggested in some quarters that students should participate in some direct and systematic way in the evaluation of individual faculty members for continuation or advancement in salary or rank. The suggestion implies a degree of dissatisfaction with existing personnel procedures in an institution which appears to be exceptional. Experience indicates that students may occasionally question an obviously unfortunate appointment, but this is far different from a desire to share in the responsibility for an across-the-board comparison of all faculty personnel as individuals, which involves a great deal more than expressing a reaction to a professor's lectures in a particular course. The issue turns on the level of competence and the degree of responsible concern which the majority of students would bring to a judgment of the effectiveness of a particular teacher except at the extremes of dullness or brilliance, or of indifference or sustained concern. The teacher is engaged in a professional service not too dissimilar from that of a doctor or a lawyer. Liberal education, in particular, involves long run results in the participant which he may not be able to foresee. Further, the art of teaching is a personal one, and diverse methods may obtain equally good results. Both subjects and personalities, even within a single discipline, lead to a blending of approaches which is far more educational than any standard, "ideal" pattern, especially one determined by a young person who may be, at times, more immediately concerned with his easy adjustment and progress in a particular course than with his total preparation for life.

An additional limitation upon the student as judge of a member of a faculty is that a departmental faculty in a liberal university is engaged in teaching at many levels, from freshman introductory courses to advanced graduate seminars, and at the same time is engaged in scholarship and research vitally necessary to sustaining tone and a sense of contribution. The student in a particular course views the teacher in but one facet of his activity. A department and a university in judging a member must weigh all dimensions, including success in various kinds and at various levels of teaching, his relative maturity, and his potentialities for growth in general and in his special field. The supply of mature, balanced, highly articulate, but intensely creative teacher-scholars is all too limited to permit a department to satisfy the predispositions of the average student in a wide battery of specialties. A department is fortunate if it has a number of teachers who are especially successful in widely elected courses. To build a department around a norm most satisfactory to the respondents on a casually checked questionnaire would be an abrogation of professional responsibility.

If there are advantages in the anonymous rating of faculty members by students, they are more than offset if the resultant gradings are published. A confidential source of guidance to those responsible for a constructive personnel program then takes on the attributes of a popularity poll. Faculty members are more likely than most to be sensitive and introspective people. They are not television stars. Applause is always pleasing, whether deserved or not. Statistically compounded censure by one's students is deeply discouraging when read in the morning paper, even if discounted for limited competency or lack of appreciation of one's intent. Few ministers, doctors, or lawyers would like to have their professional "batting average," as determined by polls of parishioners, patients, or clients, announced periodically for all to see. Even if anonymous gradings of teachers by their students were highly accurate within their limited area of competence, their use should be strictly confined to those who can use them constructively and humanely. There are many better ways to help students in planning their educational programs.

In a four-year, residential, undergraduate program in a liberal university, an essential part of the educational process is that which develops through the interaction of young persons of high potential with each other. The years from eighteen to twenty-two are a period in the life of most young people when values, aspirations, and intellectual tone become firmly established. Teachers, counselors, coaches, and deans may have great influence. The traditions of a campus do come through in some more or less subtle way. But the daily life of the student affords more contacts with fellow students than with any other group of people. The influence of the older student upon the younger student is more persistent and less resisted than that of any parent substitute. It is a well-tested premise that values are more readily communicated by assumptions than by preachments.

Several corollaries may be drawn from the conclusion that student interaction is very important in a liberal university. It suggests, again, the importance of wise admission policies which give weight to much more than academic ratings. Further, it implies that the prospective student should be fully advised of the character and personality of the university and of its students, so that he can determine whether he will find it an environment both stimulating and sympathetic given his concept of a satisfying way of life. There is a justification for the admission, without apology, of a reasonable proportion of alumni sons or daughters, if they are fully qualified—not to please their parents, but to help sustain the assumptions of a student body from generation to generation in some of the more subtle attributes of institutional tradition.

A precious tradition in a liberal university is that of dedication to public service. It assumes that young people are not educated merely to make money or to be happy, but to serve and, if occasion offers, to lead their fellow men. It is difficult to put one's finger on the precise sources or the sustaining charge in such a tradition, but it is communicated in a very important degree from older to younger students as they move through college. The tradition can be reinforced in many ways, but the ongoing communication of student assumptions, class by class, should never be discounted.

The process of communication of tradition between student generations becomes more difficult in an institution in which students come late or leave early in respect to the normal four-year span. Transfer students enter in midstream in the flow of student intercommunication. Three-year graduates, because of acceleration and more intensive concern for their studies, lose not only a culminating year in the process, but some of the opportunity for interchange which comes outside of one's courses. If liberal education is to be effective in all aspects of student development, it should be worth the investment of four years in the lengthening normal span of life. Those who argue for acceleration or other "efficient" systems of higher education tend to emphasize the accumulation of knowledge and skills and to discount or ignore the basic purpose of liberal education—to develop human beings to their highest potential.

The question may be raised: How much of the foregoing discussion applies to the ever-increasing proportion of graduate students in the liberal university? An answer based on long experience is: far more than is usually assumed. The graduate student is older and professionally oriented. But he is still in an intensely learning stage of life. As a junior colleague in a learned profession, he is likely to be more influenced by senior professors in his chosen discipline than are undergraduates. But he is also thrown in with fellow students with marked common interests. Extracurricular activities such as undergraduates find exciting are replaced by hours of discussion of the problems studied. In the framework of a liberal university, dedication, values, and assumptions should come through, since there is little use of sharpening the intellect of a physicist or classicist without deepening his sense of purpose or broadening his understanding of what is good. Again, the process is greatly helped by the daily contacts of the common life outside the classroom, library, or laboratory which a residential university provides. To house graduate students, whether married or not, in scattered rooming houses and apartments without some means of common association may be an emergency solution, but it reduces the opportunity for learning from one's peers, which is a vital part of a liberal education.

7

THE
ALUMNI

It may be surprising to some readers that the alumni as such should be included as a constituent element in the organization of a university. Are not the alumni the completed products of an educational process whose connection with the university has ended except in terms of nostalgic sentiment or partisan pride in winning teams? While such ties to one's alma mater are almost universal, given the American temperament, there appears to be a more solid basis for inclusion of the alumni among those who have an interacting influence in the life of a university of the kind which is herein examined. While the factors are clearer in the case of the older, private, liberal university, they appear in varying degree in public institutions which have come to reflect in the climate of their campuses what has been premised as a liberal approach in higher education.

It is in the nature of a truly liberal university that it is concerned with human beings first, and with knowledge and wisdom second. It is in the nature of human personality that an individual becomes attached to and involved in the life of another person or institution which has shown concern for him, not as a part of a group alone, but as an individual. This has been shown in many human institutions, from the family and the church to the party organization of a city ward or a veteran marine corps battalion. With the great growth of population and of crowded cities and suburbs, the desire of people for mutual concern on an *individual* basis seems to have become greater rather than less.

Four years of life at a formative period of development can build a firm foundation for continuing mutual concern if the environment for that experience includes many interpersonal relationships with teachers, fellow students, coaches, counselors, and even deans. Values and aspirations are best communicated where people know and respect each other as individuals. This mutual respect becomes enhanced by the continuance of cherished associations with people and with a place. A rich experience during a formative period of life becomes for many not merely a nostalgic memory, but a treasured and influential factor in their lives.

A liberal university thus forms the attitude and concern of its alumni as individuals—and therefore as a body—not so much by its flow of communication to them *after* graduation as by its concern for them as students *during* their life on campus. Since the latter is discussed elsewhere in this analysis, the comments which follow are related to post-graduation relationships. It is believed that the complex of interactions outlined will justify the inclusion of the alumni as a valuable and influential element in the total life of a liberal university.

The more usual and more formal channel for the exercise of alumni influence is through the membership of alumni on the board of trustees. Whether by election by a self-perpetuating board on its own nomination or by election through some systematic plan of nomination and voting by the alumni body, the alumnus on the board is in a position to help sustain and revise the purposes of the institution with the added insight of a former student. It is important, however, that he remember that once he has assumed office, he is no longer a representative of anyone, but a part of a legally constituted body with heavy responsibilities for the sustained welfare of the institution. The fuller knowledge of problems which comes with informed discussion, and the sobering effect of authority to deal with them, is likely to temper the *ex parte* opinions so freely expressed at alumni gatherings.

An additional channel of alumni advice and support is that of the departmental or functional advisory council, whether concerned with instruction and scholarship in philosophy, history, or chemical engineering or in the chapel, the library, or athletics. If the normally annual sessions are well planned and the terms of reference kept clear, such advisory councils can be both productive of ideas and practical support and a means of broadening the sense of participation of hundreds of alumni.

As with the board of trustees, the meeting of an advisory council requires the chairman or administrator to review and evaluate experience, to discuss problems frankly, and to present plans in a way that a visiting committee can understand. This of itself has a wholesome effect, supplemented by discussion with concerned people whose questions and comments are of value despite the absence of any authority to control policy. Advisory councils, whether limited to alumni or not, are a valuable adjunct in an institution in which response is important. But response, to be significant, must be that of qualified persons and based on adequate information. There must be an investment of time and energy in the wise selection of the membership, in the careful planning of sessions and arrangements, and in the preparation of an interesting, informative agenda in order for worthwhile results to be obtained. Without such investment, advisory councils produce very small returns.

In an institution which seeks to educate students for responsible leadership, alumni who are themselves leaders in their communities are in a strategic position to interest and evaluate young persons who would most profit by liberal education. In earlier years, there was much concern on the part of faculty members that alumni would be much more interested in a good quarterback than a good mathematician. But in this, as in other respects, a university creates the assumptions of the alumnus while he is an undergraduate. If a liberal university has made clear its basic purpose in education during a four-year period, it can trust thousands of its alumni to communicate its purposes to young candidates. "Schools and scholarship" committees of alumni scattered over the country can be of great help in sustaining the flow of highly qualified applicants. With careful selection, sustained instruction through consultation and conferences, and understanding communication on the results of their efforts, such committees can be extremely useful in the process of admissions. Again, the terms of reference indicating that such committees are advisory must be kept clear. A good committee of mature and experienced alumni can provide a judgment on the qualities of a young candidate which no tests or grades can measure. Combined with all other information, committee evaluations can markedly improve the final and responsible decision of the admissions office. In sum, it may be said that alumni do have a justifiable interest in influencing the flow of their successors, provided they are willing to take on the job responsibly yet without claiming the authority which the university must retain.

The financial support of liberal education comes most readily from those who understand liberal education. The alumni of a liberal university have more than faith alone in its effectiveness. They experience its rewards in their lives and careers. Therefore, they have reason to want to make a return for the advantages they received and to make those advantages available to others. The alumni of a liberal university should, therefore, be in the first line of those who are concerned with its financial welfare. While many, especially younger graduates, are not in a position to provide large sums in dollars, they are able to convince others, from within their numbers or outside, by their example in sustained and widespread giving.

The development of organized, annual giving programs among the alumni of older, private universities was a blessed invention. As it has matured, it has served several valuable purposes. First, it has provided current flows of funds at a time when endowment income has become increasingly inadequate in meeting rising budgets. Second, it has emphasized the importance of funds free of specification as to use, so that they could be assigned to the improvement of faculty salaries, to the support of new educational ventures, or to the renovation of a dormitory. Third, organized annual giving has brought hundreds or even thousands of alumni into a practical, ongoing relationship with the university in an area where hard work shows results and gives clear-cut satisfactions. Fourth, and finally, in those institutions where class organization by year of graduation has become an important element in institutional loyalty in social terms, it has balanced the competition to have the most members back at a five year reunion with that to make a superior showing in the annual giving results. An appeal for funds does not of itself enhance loyalty. But the giving of support when loyalty exists, both to an institution and to a class, reinforces that sense of loyalty through effective participation in a worthy cause.

Intelligent and effective participation in the life of any institution requires leadership and communication. The alumni organization of an older liberal university has become a complex system of a university staff office serving national officers and committees, which, in turn, give leadership to a dual pattern of class officers and committees and regional or local officers and committees. In some institutions, such as Princeton, the alumni class has long been the most persistent and cohesive subunit in alumni organization because of a strong tradition of class reunions at commencement and on many other occasions. Class notes in the *Alumni Weekly* assure cross-communication throughout life, and competition between classes in annual giving and special benefactions enhance pride in class.

Alumni leadership at the regional and local level has, however, come to be increasingly important as the graduates of larger institutions and the interest in both candidates for admission and financial support on the part of national institutions have spread more fully across the country. "Schools and scholarship" committees need to be in close touch with the high schools of their area in order to make individual contact with likely candidates for admission to what is often a distant and little-known university. The thoroughness with which scores of such committees carry on their canvasses and evaluate candidates on behalf of their alma mater, taken alone, would justify inclusion of alumni among the elements of university organization.

A further reason for the growth in importance of the regional organization of alumni of a private liberal university is the need for far greater support of the university through annual giving. Supplementing the appeal to class loyalty for the making of a regular and generous contribution is the more instructive effect of a personal visit by a respected fellow alumnus of the same community, well informed on university developments and needs. Competition by cities or regions in annual giving reinforces that among classes. The local committee in larger centers also serves as a convener and host when a representative of the university visits the community for a dinner or a working session.

Throughout the whole system of university-alumni relations, a need has been increasingly recognized by some institutions to communicate to alumni what the institution is *today* and what it wants to be *tomorrow* in order to build upon the understanding gained in long-past years. This can be done in part by printed material, such as the older type of alumni magazine, bulletins, and reports from the president. But, again, true communication of ideas and values is an interacting process. Since liberal education is the first business of a liberal university, the subtle and ever-evolving concept of what such education should be in a changing world must be a sustaining note in university-alumni intercommunication. It is for this reason that some universities have built balanced programs including alumni lecture-discussions on a wide range of subjects presented in distant cities and led by well-known professors; faculty-alumni seminars at times of reunions on campus or elsewhere; issues of annotated reading lists of recent books selected by professors; a newer type of quarterly magazine which reflects the breadth of concern of the liberally educated person; and monthly two- or three-day intensive sessions on campus at which selected alumni discuss policies and goals with administrators, attend undergraduate lectures, visit libraries and laboratories, and meet with students.

All these activities appear to suggest a very heavy investment in alumni relations. But, to be truly effective, they must be more than an investment seeking a direct return to the institution. They must embody the conviction that the continuing *liberal* education of an alumnus is a valuable thing for him and enhances his sensitivity to the values which have significant influence in our society. The liberal university is concerned with individuals and their dedication to leadership during more than the four years or seven years on the campus.

A more recent development in alumni relations is the effort to bring the recipients of advanced degrees into full participation in university-alumni affairs. This involves special problems, since many Ph.D.s have ties also to their undergraduate *alma mater*. Further, class affiliation is replaced by alliance with a discipline. But three or more years of close association with a group of teachers and fellow students with a lifelong, common interest is a reinforcing factor in building a continuing interest in the institution which has provided the professional basis for one's career. If the institution has shown true concern for the graduate student as a person, and not merely as a useful apprentice-teacher, the likelihood of his concern and participation in the ongoing life of the institution is greatly enhanced.

PART TWO

ISSUES
IN
ACADEMIC
POLICY

1

THE
NATURE OF
THE
EDUCATIONAL
PROCESS

There is probably more confusion and uncertainty in the minds of the general public with respect to the nature and complexities of the educational process at its various stages and in its various purposes than concerning the inherent elements of any other common experience. The confusion is more serious because it is largely unrecognized. Everyone goes through the process of gaining knowledge and skills in the early stages of education. The assumption is widespread that this is the whole fabric of education and that higher education is more of the same. The public can be excused to some extent in this autobiographical approach because of the prevalence in our inherited slogans which pass for wisdom of such expressions as "Knowledge is power." The testing procedures employed in secondary education and by industry do little to discourage the assumption.

In higher, liberal education, contrary to this common assumption, knowledge should become far more a *means* of education than an *end* in itself. One does not take a wide range of courses from art to zoology to encompass content, but primarily to utilize the differing kinds of subject matter and ways of working with each as a means of enhancing the intellectual powers and the evaluative sensitivities of one's mind. The total process of education for a person of high potential is far from simple, and, in order to indicate the place of liberal education and something of its particular characteristics and problems, it may be helpful to block out certain general considerations. It is not assumed that all will agree with this outline, since there is little precise proof of results when one is dealing with the development of human personality. The product of liberal education is a whole man, not a few attributes which happen to be measurable.

It is of special importance to define one's understanding of the nature of the educational process in a study of the liberal university. Much of what distinguishes that type of institution from many others arises from a philosophy of education which has evolved over many years and which is difficult and costly to implement on a vastly expanded scale.

The education of persons of a capacity for sustained intellectual endeavors should be, from early childhood to maturity, a changing balance—a recurring rhythm—between *education in conformity* and *education in creativity*. We must learn our language as it has come down to us, in vocabulary, spelling, and grammar. The tools and resources of mathematics, scientific analysis, historical evidence, and great literary expression are not one's own to invent. The young person must accumulate by study, analysis, and re-expression a vast stock of method and knowledge. In this, he conforms to his cultural inheritance and provides himself with the means of intelligent thought and intercommunication in the context of his society and time.

But as education progresses, especially for persons of high potential, there must be an increasing element of education in *creativity*, supplementing and building upon education in *conformity*. If the individual is to be an initiating force in his community, profession, or society, he must learn to think for himself, to use language, science, and history and all accumulating knowledge as tools and material for creative thinking and not to be tied down by someone else's thought or convictions. In brief summary:

1. He must develop a tone of attack, a climate of intellectual initiative, not critical alone, but also constructive—creative!
2. He must develop independence of mind and judgment within a framework of basic assumptions and beliefs which he comes to consider as timeless.
3. He must learn to take responsibility for his determinations in many areas—moral, esthetic, political, and social.
4. He must enhance his powers of intuition to supplement those of reason.

In the progress of education, there are repeating cycles of education in conformity (A) and education in creativity (B). This might be expressed as $A + B + A' + B'$, and so on. For example, a student preparing for law might move from languages and mathematics to politics and social philosophy, in which he does much independent thinking, and then, in law school, he must learn the conforming structures of the laws and precedents of contracts and torts as they are and not as he might believe they should be.

But in the later stages of professional education, education in creativity should again be emphasized, if leaders rather than clerks are being developed. The significant fact is that creativity at this B' stage is greatly enhanced by the presence of a B stage of creativity in earlier, undergraduate education. Properly planned education for all the learned professions and demanding occupations involves this cycle. Taken as a whole, it involves a *liberal* approach in higher education. It is true that not all universities or professions understand or uphold this view.

Creativity, as here defined, arises not as much from a command of techniques, no matter how useful, but from a climate of mind and spirit. One can, in the conformity-creativity cycle of education, start too late in introducing education in creativity and make instruction a dull drill in what the teacher considers essential. The progressive movement in American education constituted a wholesome rebellion against an overemphasis upon conformity. But, likewise, one can start too soon in emphasizing creativity at the expense of rigor in education in conformity—in learning precision in the arts of communication and in the skills of mathematical analysis, as well as in gaining a solid base for a developing appreciation of the resources of established evidence in history and of the great expressions of the human mind and spirit in literature. Education remains a discipline of the mind, and creative thought is most fruitful when it arises from ordered, analyzed knowledge rather than from rebellious ignorance.

On the basis of these considerations, it can be premised that what is needed in the education of persons for creative leadership in our society and time is balance and rhythm adjusted to the individual and his strengths and progress. A potential mathematician, scientist, or composer may have a very different rhythm and timing from a potential lawyer, businessman, or social scientist. Matching the instructional process to differing individuals and with differing timing requires not only the greater sensitivity which close contact between student and teacher provides, but a quality in the teacher which assures sympathetic adjustment. This suggests why an effective program of liberal education for leadership costs so much more in teaching talent per student than a program which is mainly confined to the transmission of knowledge and skills to large numbers of undifferentiated students.

A corollary implicit in the changing balance of education in conformity and education in creativity is the difference between information and ideas. A fact can be communicated in minutes; an idea may take years to comprehend. Information may be transmitted through books and lectures, by radio or television, or by teaching machines; an idea to be truly understood and made one's own must be hammered out on the anvil of the mind, tested and retested by analysis and discussion. Information should, so far as it is true, be objective; ideas are always in large part subjective. They become personalized concepts and instruments of thought, not merely data for an electronic computer. A technician needs, primarily, information, knowledge of techniques, and skill—"know-how." A member of a learned profession or an industrial executive needs also to have a firm comprehension of a system of ideas, values, and judgments—"know-why." Therefore, in his higher education he should have a strong liberal base which can be discounted only at a great and lasting loss. It makes the difference, if not repaired by later study, between a skilled plumber and a great physician or between a bureaucrat and a leader.

Another basic consideration in the structuring of liberal education is the balancing of breadth and depth. This is, perhaps, where the universities of the United States differ most from those in many other countries. In the older liberal universities of this country it is believed that there is a definite loss in too early and too exclusive specialization in the subject matter of education. It may well be that this is to some extent an inheritance from an earlier time when higher education in the English tradition was a preparation for life in a cultivated upper class, but it appears to remain a sound approach in a country and time when the dilettante in learning has little place. It is in present-day America a reflection of the belief that membership in a learned profession or a career in other positions of responsibility involves leadership in and dedication to a wider range of functions than specialized education alone is likely to encourage. At a more sophisticated level, it is also a reflection of an assumption of what encourages creativity as balanced against logical analysis, knowledge accumulation, and a sort of mechanistic efficiency in able individuals.

Creativity arises out of intuitive thought supported by, but not limited by, analysis and the accumulation of knowledge. Intuitive thought is stimulated by many things, some closely related to the focus of inquiry and some, apparently, far from it. It is a mysterious power of association of ideas, of bits and pieces of knowledge, of questions, hunches, and imagined premises. Intuitive thought thrives in a freewheeling climate in which sensitivity, clarity, and association work both consciously and unconsciously, and not under the severe restraints of logic or precedent. The enrichment of the mind by diverse sources of association and the stimulation of the mind by diverse approaches to understanding and appreciation seem to produce the greater results. Examples of reinforcing associations in education appear to be: music and mathematics; history and economics; literature and psychology; sociology and biology; philosophy and law; and biography and medicine. Throughout life, this matrix of cross stimuli to intuitive thought becomes a precious although often unrecognized resource to the liberally educated person when ideas or decisions involve more than logic alone.

There is in higher education particularly the need for recognition of another rhythm which is constantly at work in the minds of both student and teacher:

a. A sense of accomplishment, of a degree of mastery of knowledge, ideas, or approaches, *and*
b. A sense of humility before the great mass and complexity of that which remains unknown or not understood.

This recurring and rhythmic cycle seems always present in effective education. It is the great teacher who keeps himself aware of *both* responses in his student and reinforces them in proper proportion and timing to carry his student along to new attainment. This is far more likely to be understood by a teacher if he himself is a teacher-scholar who continues to do research. That is why teacher-scholars are needed, persons who are *both* teachers and scholars and who appreciate this cycle because they, too, are subject to it. The most corrupting influence in leadership is arrogance. To build in a self-initiating restraint upon arrogance is to provide a precious ingredient of the whole person. This is a vital concern in liberal education.

The elements in the educational process in liberal education which have been outlined will indicate why such education requires sustained interaction between the teacher and student and between the student and fellow student in order to be effective.

This, in turn, requires more opportunities for the individual student to participate in discussions with the teacher in small groups or alone. Knowledge can be dispensed in large lecture halls, but ideas and values need to be hammered out in intimate, freewheeling interchange. This is the reason effective liberal education requires more teachers in terms of the students enrolled than education emphasizing the transfer of knowledge. It also justifies the need for more mature teachers who bring more to a discussion than acquaintance with the assignment of the day.

The economic costs of truly effective higher education are so severe a limiting factor upon its extension that many educators themselves are prone to justify the possible over against the ideal. Since effective liberal education emphasizing the interactive approach can be provided for a far smaller proportion of those in the age group from eighteen to twenty-two than want to go to college these days, the exponent of higher education for all permits one value concept, egalitarianism, to confuse or becloud another value judgment: that of the true purpose of higher, liberal education.

It can be argued that every high school graduate, regardless of standing, should have the opportunity to have something properly called a college-level, liberal education. If this could be financed by an affluent society, it might appear to be a justifiable allocation of funds. But the critical question is whether the financing of such higher education on such a scale would not increasingly corrode the standards and effectiveness of higher liberal education of proven quality and of proven need in the development of those individuals who, regardless of financial resources, have high potential for leadership in a complex democratic society. The greatest danger is that the exponents of higher education for all will so confuse themselves and the public that they will pour out the baby with the bath. Americans have a distaste for differentiating processes affecting people. Effective liberal education, because of its very nature, is expensive in terms of both dollars and human talent, and must be selective. In the years ahead it may have to fight for its existence in a society which pours billions into vast lecture halls, dormitory systems, student centers, and stadiums with but limited concern for the kind of education provided.

2

ACADEMIC
FREEDOM
AND
TENURE

It is unfortunate that the concept of academic freedom in higher education comes to the attention of the public most often when some professor is accused of upholding some unpopular political cause. The concept has far deeper and wider significance than is suggested by the layman's reaction that the accused man can't be fired because professors are protected by some kind of union rule which says that they can speak or write what they please on any occasion. Rather, it goes to the heart of the total approach of liberal education in a democracy.

It has been the conclusion of wise men over the centuries that truth is sooner and more surely discovered if men are free to search for it in their own way and to defend their views and findings in open discussion. The creative scientist is more likely to discover new laws and relationships in nature if his intuition is not cribbed in by a requirement that he produce immediately useful knowledge or that he keep within certain boundaries of approved doctrine. From Galileo to Darwin, the scientist has broken away from such restraints. Even the Soviet Union and the state of Tennessee have now come to see that the intervention of government in limiting the search for truth in science is both medieval and self-defeating.

But the more difficult area in which to demonstrate the fact that freedom accelerates the search for truth is that of humane values and political and social ideas. It is here that the proof of contribution cannot be made evident and must be taken on faith. This is not, in fact, so different from the faith required of the layman when he is asked to believe that many discoveries in physics or biology are as significant as claimed. It is seldom that a formula like Einstein's results in an atomic bomb. Yet the layman feels that he knows what is right and wrong in value or policy terms, so that freedom for the humanist or the social scientist comes up against predilections which discount the contribution of the scholar and therefore question the degree of advantage to society arising from free scholarship in these fields.

Universities, and particularly the liberal universities, must uphold the concept of freedom to discover truth and to teach truth in *all* the areas they decide to cover. This is the academic freedom of the *institution* as such. Without that freedom on the part of an institution, there cannot be academic freedom for the professor. Such freedom must be a part of the personality of the institution —an ongoing tradition, reinforced by sensitive leadership and constant vigilance. This goal is easier to announce than to assure.

The freedom of an institution may be impaired in subtle but persistent ways. For centuries, abroad, the study of religion—the greatest single influence on the actions and aspirations of mankind —was assumed to be a proper field of study in the university. For many American universities, however, a venture into this field was long considered risky unless kept out of the regular curriculum or carefully placed in a separate, tenuously affiliated enclave. It was proper in a narrow sense for the university to make this decision, just as other institutions decided to terminate direct affiliation with a church; but the point is that the institution, in avoiding the study of religion as an integral part of liberal education and scholarship, was not acting like a free agent in the search for truth, but rather taking an expedient course. It is a welcome sign that more institutions have moved to add a competent coverage of comparative religion, not as professional training for ministers, but as a significant branch of learning.

The example of freedom on the part of an institution to provide for instruction and scholarship in religion reflects the uncertainty which surrounds *institutional* decisions in value terms. Of course, an institution can stand for honesty, honorable dealings, good manners, and good taste, but has it a right or an obligation to treat all persons as equals regardless of race or color? Before the imposition of constitutional requirements in recent years, an institution probably had the legal *right* to choose its faculty and students as it wished. But it is a deep conviction on the part of many that a liberal university has always faced the *obligation* to respect the common dignity of all human beings as a basic condition for true academic freedom. So long as a line of policy or action of an institution was foreclosed for political or social reasons, there could not fail to be an assumption that the free study and discussion of problems of race and color were to be questioned.

It is in the nature of intellectual activity that a restriction upon any area of thought affects not only that area, but the whole climate of thought. An institution which by rule or assumption has foreclosed any area from free study and discussion loses true academic freedom. The effect may not be obvious to the casual observer, but it is a restraining influence in the minds of teachers and students. It can be argued that self-imposed restrictions are themselves the manifestations of freedom, but the more one studies the facts, the more one becomes aware that few restrictions are really self-imposed. They are usually the consequence of subtle or overt pressures, or even rules, forthcoming from groups or agencies outside the university.

The conclusion cannot be avoided that a church-related university is in a difficult position in assuring a condition of complete academic freedom. There is no question of the right of any religious establishment to sponsor and support a college or university which respects its convictions of truth. But so long as freedom of inquiry or instruction is limited *in any area* for reasons reflecting external influence or control, true academic freedom does not exist.

This does not mean that faculties must be free to extend the curriculum in any direction they may wish, since some areas may be outside the mission of the institution as properly determined by the trustees who are responsible for sustaining the approved mission of the institution. But such limitations on curriculum are likely to affect the outer margins of more specialized or professional education and to be related to the costs which such programs may involve. For the board of trustees to make distinctions with respect to coverage *within* the normal area of arts and sciences, however, is an introduction of control within an integrated body of learning. It suggests a questionable extension of trustee influence, as well as a limitation upon true academic freedom.

It has been stated that a university must uphold a condition of academic freedom for itself in order to assure academic freedom for its teacher-scholars. In so doing it has an obligation to its students and to society to be concerned with the character as well as the intellectual competence of the persons to whom it provides the protective cloak of academic freedom. Freedom must be balanced by responsibility at all levels. Responsibility must be based upon ethical assumptions, and these are personal and not merely institutional.

Therefore, the university, and particularly the liberal university, must choose its faculty on grounds broader than technical competence in a subject alone. To justify academic freedom with responsibility, it has the right as well as the obligation to avoid hiring a teacher or scholar who is insensitive to moral standards or professional obligations. As discussed earlier, this involves the members of a department in recommending an appointment to its particular group of teacher-scholars and also the administration in reviewing such recommendations on an institutional basis. This is a further justification for a probationary period of employment for younger persons especially, where responsibility to the professional obligations of membership may still need to be tested.

While academic freedom should pervade the total institution and exist for all teacher-scholars on the faculty regardless of rank, the issue of its existence most frequently arises with respect to an ancillary mechanism designed to assure academic freedom. This is the concept of tenure. So much attention has been paid to the guarantee of tenure that the means often overshadows the end. The establishment of assumptions and, better, clearly stated rules concerning the acquiring of tenure in membership on a university faculty is an exceedingly important contribution to academic freedom for society, the institution, the individual professor, and the student. It must be emphasized again, however, that it is a supporting procedure and not an end in itself. If this is kept clear, certain issues in its implementation become clarified.

A nagging question in the implementation of the concept of tenure is, When should it be acquired? Since tenure involves a career-long commitment on the part of an institution to an individual in terms of both responsible participation in an educational enterprise and financial costs for salary and benefits, the university seeks to have sufficient time to make sure that the member is fully qualified. The member and those who assume to support his interests may push for a shorter probationary period. In balancing these positions, it must be reiterated that academic freedom does not begin with tenure, and that the institution, to properly uphold academic freedom as a total concept, must confirm its faith in the competency and professional responsibility of the individual who will enjoy its benefits. A probationary period is not just a sum of years, wherever spent, in the career of the individual. It is a part of a procedure within a particular institution to make a means— tenure—an effective supporting mechanism for academic freedom.

The liberal university, especially in the absence of rapid

growth, faces a serious problem in selecting younger teacher-scholars for tenure appointments to its faculty. Not only must there be opportunity to evaluate the candidate as a person—his character, personality, and dedication—but also to judge his potentialities as *both* teacher and scholar over the long years ahead. Further, in a university it is insufficient to know that he is, for example, a good historian. It must be determined that he is a historian whose continuing interest and contribution will be, in particular, in one of a dozen or more subfields of history for which the university needs coverage.

It is only after the younger man has completed his graduate education and attained a final degree that he is really on his own as a teacher-scholar. Experience indicates that a five-year period after attaining the Ph.D. degree may well be needed for an adequate testing of his scholarly quality, teaching effectiveness, and sustained interest in a particular subfield of study. In considering the need for a probationary period of up to five years after attainment of the Ph.D. before tenure is awarded in the faculty of a *university*, one must distinguish the conditions surrounding faculty development in a university from those concerning such development in a *college*. A university faculty must offer specialized graduate instruction and supervise advanced scholarship and research, whereas a college faculty is primarily concerned with undergraduate instruction. The five-year period is here assumed to be a probationary period for promotion to associate professor with automatic tenure, since it appears unwise to retain a faculty member who does not deserve senior status. By the end of a five-year period following attainment of the Ph.D., an assistant professor has had full opportunity to demonstrate his qualifications as both a teacher and a scholar in a subdivision of his discipline which the university needs to have covered at all levels of instruction and in which he can attain recognized standing. He has also had the opportunity to prove that he is a responsible member of a team.

The approach here proposed for the attainment of tenure by younger teacher-scholars seeking permanent appointment in a *university* combines the interest of the university in developing an able, balanced faculty and the interest of those who aspire to membership in that kind of faculty. It does not terminate the services of the candidate for tenure before he can prove himself qualified for university-level, permanent appointment. It avoids an arbitrary curtailment of the probationary period when the candidate for a tenure position in the university needs to finance his graduate education by some form of academic employment. Such employment may have been in teaching or research, part time or full time, continuous or interspersed with periods of full-time study. The university, in placing its emphasis on the period in a member's career *following* attainment of the Ph.D., avoids the arbitrary result of curtailing a probationary period because of the way a candidate for tenure financed his graduate education.

With the scarcity of young teacher-scholars of high potential, sound personnel administration supports a policy of strong encouragement of growth during the probationary period through paid leaves, research assignments, and appropriate teaching opportunities. While disciplines and individuals vary with respect to the ideal testing period, it is better for all concerned to have a firmly established, universitywide limit to avoid prolongation because of neglect, indecision, or bad planning. Progress throughout the period should be reviewed annually and especially at the end of three years. At that time, reappointment should be limited to those for whom promotion is likely, except for a terminal appointment of one year.

The foregoing discussion of policy with respect to the probationary period before the determination of tenure in a university where an effective personnel program exists has been more detailed than would be appropriate if it were in line with the principles approved by the American Association of University Professors and the American Association of Colleges more than a quarter of a century ago. While the 1940 statement of principles on "Academic Freedom and Tenure" contains an excellent outline of the purposes, nature, and means of safeguarding academic freedom and of appropriate associated procedures in respect to tenure, it includes, as a means of avoiding excessively long probationary periods, a "seven-year rule" with a provision for amendment by agreement under certain conditions of change of employment.

The limit of seven years makes no distinction, however, between service prior to attaining a Ph.D. degree and service after its attainment, so long as it is full time. A protracted period of service as a part-time teaching assistant or as a research assistant in science does not count, but a year as a full-time instructor in English to help finance one's graduate work counts wherever one is employed.

In light of the great changes which have occurred in the conditions of graduate study in this country and in those affecting the development of strong and specialized faculties in the modern university, it is believed that a probationary period related to *post-Ph.D.* service in the university which will make a lifelong commitment to the member has become reasonable and beneficial for all parties. The 1940 "seven-year rule" may be applicable to employment in colleges where the Ph.D. is not required for appointment to the assistant professor rank, but a five-year, post-Ph.D. rule would be a more constructive support of academic freedom in a university. If implemented, it would also serve to encourage universities to improve their programs of personnel development and of evaluation of the precious younger talent upon which their future progress depends.

Tenure, as an effective means of assuring academic freedom, assumes that the individual on tenure continues to be, in general, the kind of person he was during the period in which he held probationary status. It is obvious that, if he becomes permanently disabled or reaches the established age of retirement, tenure ceases. (It is assumed that the institution provides financial protection against these personal contingencies.) For the type of universities herein discussed, the likelihood of an institution's inability to meet its financial obligations to professors on tenure is too slight to warrant concern. Two other contingencies in the long career of the member deserve consideration, however, as possible justifications for terminating tenure status. They are (*a*) a marked decline in professional competence or performance and (*b*) personal conduct which unfits the person for participation in a teaching community.

Whatever the legal rights of the institution may be or how

surely dismissal would be supported under a most conscientious exercise of due process, it appears to be the counsel of wisdom to avoid, to the fullest extent possible, terminations of tenure related to professional competency. The university is assumed to have had an adequate opportunity to evaluate the individual. Some individuals fail to respond to the changing demands of their discipline. On average, mistakes in judgment of human potential are bound to occur.

The university should, it is believed, make the best accommodation it can when mistakes have been made, as a contribution to the overall advantage of assuring security of tenure as a safeguard to academic freedom, and as a support to good human relations. It should do everything possible to salvage the member and its investment in him by appropriate adjustment of work assignments and by providing opportunities for professional rehabilitation. Only in the limiting case of overt refusal to perform such adjusted work assignments as are deemed appropriate by both his colleagues and the administration should termination or early retirement be considered. The right of hearing and the procedures of due process should be fully respected. In such cases, it is advisable to obtain medical or psychiatric advice, if there is any suggestion of physical or mental impairment.

Any termination of tenure on grounds of incompetency should involve adequate financial compensation by the institution. This is a sound industrial relations policy as well as a "repurchase of contract." Where a younger person finds himself in the wrong profession while there is still a chance to change, a confidential offer of generous compensation on termination may be a worthwhile investment for the institution and a valuable stimulus to the person to make a mutually beneficial move. Like other strong measures, however, it is a step to be taken only after most conscientious study, since it could become a tempting subterfuge in getting rid of an unpopular troublemaker. The best guide to judgment is: what is best for the man, whether he realizes it or not, is best for the institution.

The most difficult area of administrative decision with respect to the termination of tenure is that relating to personal conduct which may disqualify the person for participation in a teaching community. A teacher influences his students by his approach to life as well as by his approach to learning. Academic freedom and membership in a dedicated profession impose a degree of personal responsibility to one's colleagues and students, as well as to one's institution, which is more demanding than that necessarily accepted by the man in the street. Irresponsibility may develop through weakness, moral obtuseness, or overt refusal to accept the standards of decent behavior recognized in one's community.

Every institution must, over time, come to some working assumptions of what particular departures from personal responsibility constitute sufficient reason for reprimand, warning, suspension, or termination of appointment. There is no prohibition under academic freedom or tradition against a president, a dean, or a chairman reprimanding a faculty member who has brought his profession and institution into disrepute. The issue for the administrator is whether the offense arises from a persistent defect in personality or character, a regretted error in judgment, or conditions which can be removed through medical treatment. Especially in the case of the first of these causes, the administrator, once convinced, must take drastic action to protect the health and good name of his institution.

It is most difficult to establish in advance what constitutes sufficient cause for dismissal where personal standards of behavior are involved. Since the obligations of a profession are the nub of the matter, and not the policing of potential delinquents, it is better to avoid any set rules and to rely upon a most conscientious consideration of the individual case with the safeguards of due-process procedures. It is well to remember, however, that professional standards in an ongoing institution are the primary consideration and not the personal predilections of a righteously indignant dean or a more tolerant chairman. It is for this reason that confidential consultation with a delinquent member's senior colleagues is a wise step, if there is any doubt.

But, in the end, the president must resolve each issue concerning termination in *institutional* terms and be ready to support his action, if appealed. He has a right, therefore, to be constantly concerned with a sensitive evaluation of the moral responsibility of those recommended to him for tenure, either by promotion or by outside appointment. It is unfortunate but true that early doubts concerning a candidate's sensitivity to obligation tend to increase, rather than decrease, through time. Academic freedom and institutional integrity of purpose are too precious to risk through carelessness or easy tolerance in the awarding of tenure.

3

THE
RELATION
OF TEACHING
AND
RESEARCH

The confusion on the part of the general public concerning the place of research in the modern university arises out of a misunderstanding of the educational process, on the one hand, and of the nature of the professor who guides that process, on the other. Effective liberal education, on the part of the student, is the process of seeking truth and understanding at his level of comprehension. Effective teaching is leadership in that process. Such teaching can best be done by a person who is engaged in the process himself and whose tone, enthusiasm, and sustained motivation to both learn and teach are a reflection of this lifelong engagement.

If higher education were merely the transfer of knowledge from one man to another, some persons could be assigned to the production of new knowledge and others to the transfer of the product to the consumer in packages of appropriate design. This would be a proper division of labor in a soap business. But in higher education such a division of function fails to recognize that knowledge is but the *means* of education and not its end. The end is what happens to the student as a thinking, judging, active person and not as a storehouse of facts. Even for the teacher-scholar, knowledge is a *means* for discovery, rather than its end. Higher education in a university is a closely integrated continuum from which learning, teaching, and scholarship can be separated out as distinct elements only at the expense of the vitality of the total mission.

It is true, of course, that many teacher-scholars are not neatly balanced in their effectiveness as teachers and as research scholars. Some teachers do well in elementary courses because of a gift for adjusting pace and method to younger minds. This gift is not impaired by effectiveness in research, although research activity may limit the time and effort available for teaching. Other teachers are most effective in advanced courses or in the guiding of graduate students in their learning through research. A problem arises when a professor becomes so involved in his own research that he has neither time nor interest in the development of young minds except as useful assistants to him. But it is also a distorted balance in the teacher-scholar if his zeal for discovery deteriorates and he resorts to oversimplification and well-worn expositions of his subject to cover his declining excitement. Discovery does not always mean the uncovering of new knowledge for the world. To have its effect on the tone of the teacher, it must, at least, involve new insights and deeper understanding for him.

The principle that a university teacher should be an active scholar should not be discounted because it is difficult to assure that an ideal balance exists in every individual appointed. It is sound policy to avoid appointments at either extreme, however, and to seek that blending of personnel which provides the best overall balance possible in each discipline. In a university department which has developed a strong tradition for both good teaching and good scholarship, the member who avoids his share of either function becomes a cause for dissatisfaction among his colleagues. Either others must take on more than their share of teaching duties, or the department loses in the outside recognition which the results of scholarship usually enhance. Only on rare occasions is the appointment of a distinguished scholar with very limited teaching duties an effective measure unless he is needed as a catalytic agent for the stimulation of his colleagues as much as of the students he may teach.

Even though balance may be attained in a discipline by the blending of individuals of diverse tendencies, the decision to appoint always concerns a single person. If the appointment is to a junior rank, there is an opportunity to check the assumed potentialities of the individual in regard to teaching and scholarship before tenure is granted. Since tenure involves a career commitment, it is understandable that those who sit in judgment seek all the evidence they can obtain on indications of both teaching effectiveness and scholarly insight and momentum. Evidence of the former is usually more readily available. It is in respect to the latter attributes—scholarly insight and momentum—which assure the powers of regeneration and growth over long years ahead, that most debate occurs, both among those charged with the decision and those who are concerned with the result.

It is when decisions are made against promotion or reappointment to tenure because of doubts in respect to the scholarly attributes of a candidate that the expression "publish or perish" gains currency. There is probably no aspect of faculty administration which is more certain to arouse public criticism than the issue crudely distilled in this phrase. The misunderstanding of the very important role of publication in the evaluation of creative men lies in the shift from ends to means. To the public, and to the eventual user of knowledge, whether in academia or in industry, the published book or article stands as a contribution in itself. To the peer group within the university and to the central administration, the publication is a valuable means of gaining insight into the creative powers, tone of attack, self-discipline, balanced judgment, and sustained motivation of the author. Books and articles are only one means of "entering" a man's mind, but they have the important attribute that, through widespread distribution, they can be read critically by large numbers of people not influenced by personal association with the author. Also, in the words of Bacon, "writing maketh an exact man." Errors or sloppiness which can be covered up in oral discussion become apparent in the written statement. It is not the amount of writing, but the quality and insight shown in writing, which should be evaluated. The momentum of publication by the potentially creative teacher-scholar is affected by many factors, but an insignificant flow from the spring suggests doubts concerning the vitality of the source.

Not all disciplines lend themselves to major dependence upon publication as the test of scholarly momentum. In some areas, such as public affairs, many contributions to knowledge and understanding which involve scholarly insight are joint products in which individual authorship is submerged. Also, some scholars, as they mature, find their greatest satisfaction in stimulating colleagues and students by contributing the germs of new ideas for them to nourish and perfect. Criticism, based on scholarship, is an evidence of scholarship. Occasionally a scholar of high potential transmits most of his hard-won wisdom through consultation with others. The best approach in dealing with men of diverse talents and inclinations is to seek to judge their creativity and momentum as scholars on an individual basis, looking for any and all manifestations of tone and motivation. It must be argued, however, regardless of the easy taunt of "publish or perish," that the teacher-scholar who seeks an appointment on assured tenure for decades ahead should stand the close scrutiny of the other means of communication he may prefer if he seldom puts the results of his scholarship into print where all can read.

The careful consideration which must be given to scholarly potential in the selection of younger men for promotion to tenure puts an obligation on the university to provide adequate opportunity for them to develop their scholarly abilities. An ideal plan is to assure each assistant professor at least one term with salary without teaching in every three years for more intensive study or research. This appears to be a heavy expense, which few institutions can afford, but in the building of a strong faculty for many years ahead, it is a wise investment. Not only are young teacher-scholars encouraged to maintain their drive in scholarship after completion of their doctoral thesis, but now being on their own, they can be better evaulated as self-reliant scholars. The elimination of some who cannot effectively respond to the challenge of an extended period for research is, of itself, a valuable aid in assuring a strong faculty. An extension of the concept of leaves for scholarship for younger men is a provision for a full year off for study for those of unusual promise. By careful selection of those granted this special privilege, young men of exceptional talent are accelerated in their scholarly careers.

A university's investment in leaves for scholarship as a means of assuring the sustained effectiveness of the teacher-scholars on its faculty cannot be limited to younger men. The older concept of a "sabbatical" leave as an element in the employment contract now appears obsolete in two respects. First, the acceleration in the growth of knowledge in most disciplines today makes a period of seven years far too long for the active scholar in his rhythm of part-time and full-time application to study and writing. Second, the assumption that the time off is an attractive privilege of interest mainly to the professor and a periodic long vacation for the replenishment of his energies and his general well-being has been replaced by that of the common concern of both the institution and the member with his continuing effectiveness as a teacher-scholar. The institution should provide leaves for scholarship more frequently, ideally every three to four years. At the same time, it has a right to know that such an expensive investment of duty time will be appropriately employed. This should involve the submission to the departmental chairman of a statement concerning the project of scholarship planned, which, approved by him, can be reviewed by the appropriate dean.

To afford flexibility in the assignment of paid leaves for scholarship for tenure members of a faculty, a system of departmental quotas of such leaves appears preferable to the use of stated intervals between leaves for each member. Not only do individuals have a varying need for leaves, but the concept that a paid leave is a joint investment related to an approved use militates against a common fixed period for all. Such regularity in assignment carries over too much of the concept that a paid leave is a fringe benefit for which all are equally eligible regardless of the probable contribution to the member's effectiveness as a teacher-scholar.

If balancing the activity of a university faculty between teaching and scholarship were left to the faculty and administration of the university without outside influences, it would be far more easily attained. Since World War II, however, a new factor has affected the balance, particularly in science and engineering. The increasing interest of the federal government in research and the availability of large sums from federal agencies have put pressure upon universities to release more of the time of their faculties in these fields for research—not for self-improvement alone, but to maintain a flow of new knowledge of possible advantage to national security or strength. While it has always been assumed that research is, over time, a source of beneficial knowledge, the entrance of the government into the field, assigning large sums of taxpayers' money, has added a new dimension to the issue of how much research activity can be supported within a university without distorting the general mission of effective higher education.

The control of research activities as an element in university administration will be discussed later. The issue at this point is: How much of a professor's time should be assigned to research without impairment of his role as a teacher-scholar? A workable rule appears to be that the assignment of more than half time, in terms of normal teaching schedules, to research during the academic year and apart from the summer period or leaves is excessive in most fields, if the balance and momentum of instruction at all levels are to be maintained. Most universities can afford to give tenure to but a limited number of members in a given discipline and must spread such appointments over the major subareas covered. To have some professors on research assignment for more than a half-time schedule not only puts pressure upon the institution's ability to provide effective instruction without inflating tenure manning beyond a safe level over time, but departs from the principle that research in a university is justified by its valuable effects upon the professor and his teaching. While the individual professor may prefer a heavy preoccupation with research which redounds to his standing in his field, the institution must assure fulfillment of its whole mission and, particularly, the assurance of a continuing flow of high talent for society.

It is true that in some areas of rapidly growing knowledge the precise line between instruction and research has become less clear. In fields such as aeronautical engineering and plasma physics, an appropriate method of instruction may be participation in joint research endeavors. The equipment and facilities required may be both elaborate and expensive. The test remains, however, in the purpose of the endeavor. If the professor in charge of the research project is looking primarily for results which can be reported to justify a new contract and only secondarily for means of developing his students, a departure from sound balance has occurred.

The need of the government for vigorous and extensive programs of research cannot be denied. But the role of the liberal university is clear. It must protect itself as the source of the scientists and research engineers for the long future. The kind of research which fits its mutually reinforcing mission of education and scholarship is *fundamental* research under conditions of true academic freedom. The test is what is good for the professor as an effective teacher-scholar and thereby good for the students under his charge.

Apart from the university, two types of institution have arisen in which scholarship and research are the exclusive, or almost exclusive, mission. The one type is the institute for advanced study, where advanced or mature scholars carry on their work with great freedom yet without the consumption of time or energy in organized instruction. The other is the research organization supported by government or corporate funds to carry on research assumed to be of interest, sooner or later, to the sponsor. In a pluralistic society there is room for a variety of agencies whose mission is the pursuit of knowledge. But the separation of the function of scholarship and research from that of teaching does not seem to be as productive over the long pull as a mutually reinforcing combination. This is especially true for the enthusiastic and dynamic scholar who finds deep satisfaction in leading others to develop their powers of mind and spirit. Teaching and scholarship are an interacting process in which tone is enhanced by that interaction. Concentration upon research may be a necessary condition for some agencies of government in a time of world tensions, but it is believed that neither of the types of institution which have been described will go far as a substitute for the university. A few places may be convenient havens for the professor on leave, but to this extent they are more nearly adjuncts of a university system that pioneers in a new approach to learning.

While the pressures to shift the balance of effort on the part of faculty members from teaching to research in science and engineering, and to some extent in certain social sciences, have been generated externally by national interest and support, there have developed in recent years internal pressures within the humanities to expand the scope of creative activity on the part of the teacher-scholar. This has been the trend for some professors to move from concentration on historical scholarship toward creative endeavor in the arts and literature. The argument has been that the teacher of art, music, or literature is better able to help his students to gain insight in these fields if, as teacher-scholar, he is more fully aware of the circumstances which influence the creative process in himself. In these terms, the argument parallels that for all areas of learning: that the effective teacher must have the urge and opportunity to discover in order to sustain his tone of attack in leading others, his students, to discover new truths for themselves.

This justification for extending the opportunity for the professor in a liberal university to be a creative person in the art form in his field, and not a scholarly critic alone, does not imply that the university has become a conservatory or a haven for professional writers. The teacher-scholar in art, music, or literature who holds a permanent professorship has that position in a university for the same basic reason that a professor of physics does: to help maintain a flow of talented persons to meet the needs of society. There is need for both elementary and advanced instruction in the subject as a significant discipline. If the professor becomes merely a coach in developing in others skills in performance alone, whether on the cello, the stage, or the basketball court, he ceases to be a teacher-scholar. If he uses the knolwedge and insights gained in his own creative activity in a field of art to lead others to greater insights, he remains a teacher-scholar as the term is here employed.

Since relatively few professors who have come up through the usual graduate program leading to the Ph.D. degree are predisposed to creative activity in the art form of their discipline, many universities find that the climate for such creative work is enhanced by the presence on campus of writers, artists, and composers or of persons trained in the direction of artistic performance. Such persons have a valuable function in serving to enrich the understanding of both teachers and students of the creative process in their fields.

The line between liberal education and professional training is, however, difficult to draw, especially in the liberal university. The best test of how far to move toward the introduction of practitioners of any of the arts into the educational program depends more upon the attitude of the practitioner toward his students than upon his professional background. If he seeks to enhance in his students an understanding, a sensitivity to values, and a feeling for the relations of his art to human aspirations in general, he reinforces the contribution of the teacher-scholars with whom he is associated. He thus becomes, in a sense, a teacher-scholar-practitioner similar to a professor of architecture or engineering. If he confines himself to training his students in the techniques of an art, he becomes a coach. The effective coach can contribute greatly in many areas of human activity and development, but the distinction between the teacher-scholars who form the core of the faculty in a liberal university and the coaches who assist individuals to gain specialized skills whether in painting or in football should be clearly defined. To merge all types of personnel into a supposedly homogeneous faculty creates confusion in both mission and responsibility for its fulfillment. While some coaches as individuals may be both excellent teachers and highly effective counselors of young persons, the easy assignment of faculty status is not the proper recognition of their special function in the university.

4

CONSULTING
AND
PUBLIC
SERVICE

In a time of accelerating change in almost all aspects of American life and in our nation's responsibilities throughout the world, the obligations of a liberal university can no longer be confined to the education of youth and the advancement of knowledge. New knowledge, new ideas, and new considerations in values are too essential to the welfare of a dynamic society to await their transmission through each newly educated generation of students or through publication in books and specialized journals. Further, the leading universities of the country have attracted to their faculties many of those best fitted to communicate and interpret, through interactive consultation, the knowledge and ideas which others must implement. The question is not whether this expanded role of direct communication is now thrust upon the university, but how the university will fulfill this added mission without impairing its effectiveness in the education of young persons or in creative fundamental scholarship and research.

The nub of the problem facing the university is: balancing the activities of its faculty—the cutting edge of the university—between teaching, scholarship, and ventures in the outside world. In practical terms, this is the problem of determining sound policies concerning part-time consulting or detached service for limited periods with government agencies, corporations, or other organizations in need of specialized knowledge or talent, at home or abroad. The university cannot permit itself to become, through passive tolerance or ineffective administration, a "livery stable" of talent available for hire. It is not only the quality and integrity of a complex system of educational programs which are involved, but the equitable and productive assignment of the time and energy of the university's most precious resource, its faculty. The stronger a faculty, the more necessary a carefully developed and wisely administered policy becomes. Able scientists, engineers, and social scientists are in great demand, particularly those who have the advantage of the experience, intellectual resources, and independence which come with senior, tenure status in a dynamic university. The goal in policy is to assure that outside activities will enhance the effectiveness of a strong faculty *within* the university in its *primary* missions of teaching and scholarship.

In a statement of policy on consulting or detached service by members of a faculty, it appears proper to present, as a preamble, the basic purposes recognized by the university for such activity. A possible summary of such purposes might be:

    a. To enrich the experience and understanding of the teacher-scholar by exposure to the problems of implementing theoretical principles in the complex and demanding conditions of industry, government, or public affairs and thereby to enhance his effectiveness as a teacher-scholar.

b. To provide a channel of communication whereby knowledge and judgment gained in scholarly pursuits may be of service to the nation and the world, not limited to the sole advantage of a single firm or institution.

In the further explanation of policy, it should be made clear that, in the determination of the propriety of any arrangement for consulting or detached service, the basic aims outlined should be the paramount consideration, subject to the ability of the faculty member to provide the time and energy required without impairment of the effective fulfillment of his obligations within the university. It is a wise policy for the university administration, in order to emphasize purpose and personal obligation rather than financial considerations, to avoid reference to the amount of outside compensation received. The value of a professor's services within the university and the time and energy required to fulfill them cannot be assessed in common terms with those for outside consulting. An outstanding scientist or engineer may receive from an industrial corporation a very generous fee for an experience which is valuable to him and which requires but little diversion of time and energy. A junior faculty member, however, needing funds badly, may be tempted to give much too much time on a "sweatshop" basis without gaining truly useful experience. In no case should compensation for part-time consulting by a faculty member on full-time university duty be considered an offset to an equitable salary rate within the university. If a professor is slighting his university obligations, there are better remedies than triming off a small part of his pay.

Outside consulting or other outside employment, including part-time teaching, should not duplicate the normal functions of a faculty member on full-time appointment within the university.* Such parallel activity merely adds to the duties performed by the member without significant enrichment of experience or understanding. Arrangements for outside consulting or other employ-

* An exception to this general policy may be justified in the case of assistance to a neighboring university on a temporary basis when the latter is unable to maintain instruction in a specialized field because of illness or other emergency.

ment should be discussed with the chairman of the member's department to assure both the chairman and the member himself that such activity does not interfere with his responsibilities within the department or the university, but rather, in each case, complements and enhances the member's effectiveness as a member of the faculty.

Since the best allocation of the teacher-scholar's time and effort is a matter of judgment and varies so much with discipline, personal development, and the character of the outside endeavor, the combined judgment of both the member and the chairman should be involved in any continuing arrangements. While the chairman may be hesitant to veto proposed arrangements, he should bring his judgment to bear, particularly with younger men, since he will be influential in determining the future salary and rank of the member. To allow a colleague to involve himself in excessive outside activity without firm warning and then to penalize him in terms of university status or compensation does not seem to be either fair dealing or responsible leadership. If the chairman needs advice on universitywide precedents, he can consult with the appropriate dean.

This does not mean that all persons will respond to good advice. Some, under pressure of financial need or because of excessive enthusiasm for practical affairs, may through diversion of time, energy, and interest from the main mission of the teacher-scholar prove to themselves and their colleagues over time that they do not belong in a university. That an individual would himself come to the decision to leave the university may seem questionable to those who have not experienced the subtle influences of colleague opinion in the way of life of an academic department. Tradition and consensus with respect to personal obligation are the precious attributes of a strong faculty.

The discussion of the measures which may be taken to control excessive involvement of faculty members in outside activities may give the impression that it is suggested that the university should take a generally negative position in terms of its obligation to fulfill its expanding role in society. This is not intended. It is a long-observed condition, however, that the initiative to take on outside activities comes normally, in each particular instance, from the individual faculty member. The pressures today are to move outward. In the countervailing tensions of a dynamic institution, the administration must exercise most of its influence upon preserving the integrity of the university in its continuing and principal mission. The university cannot deny the growing importance of communicating new knowledge, new ideas, or value judgments to the world through consulting or similar methods; but in that complex and sensitive organism called a university, it must, at least in a time when outside activity is as exciting as it is today, assure restraint. Communication of this kind must remain a by-product, even though one of great value to society. The university cannot permit the outflow to dry up the spring.

A different but less usual problem faced by a university is that of requests for extended leaves for senior professors for duty with a govenmental agency. Requests from government are likely to be buttressed by strong assurances of the great contribution of the individual and the university to the public interest should he perform the mission proposed. The best policy appears to be to restrict such leaves to temporary duty in virtually unique positions in government where the special knowledge or insights of the member are clearly required and not merely his attributes as a generally effective person. Such leaves should be limited to one year to avoid both the loss of momentum of the member's teaching program and to reduce the subtle temptation for him to seek the best of two careers. Only in the most exceptional situations, involving the highest levels of government, should a leave be extended to two years. By this time, even a distinguished member of a faculty should decide where his career lies.

It is the university's mission to produce many future candidates for responsible positions in government. It cannot continue to perform this function if it impairs its capacity to teach. Also, the university professor who becomes responsible for governmental policy over an extended period tends to lose in some degree the persistent power of concentration and the free wheeling critical approach of the academic scholar, even though this loss may be offset in part by greater understanding of the political forces which affect public policy.

A special problem arises where government service, especially abroad, requires the faculty member to accept a predetermined posture in respect to government policy or to restrict his freedom in the use of the knowledge gained. The wisest course appears to be to discourage mixing academic freedom and political expediency, no matter how much such a mixture is justified in the minds of those in official positions. In time of great national emergency, the professor should serve his country by every means at his command. Except in such an emergency, his contribution is likely to be greater in his chosen career. Academic freedom is itself an essential source of national strength over time. A teacher-scholar of high potential should not impair it for himself or blur its meaning for others for the sake of interesting excursions into activities involving conflicting assumptions.

With the recognized need to assist developing countries throughout the world, some universities have assumed an institutional obligation to provide leadership and instruction in a particular university abroad. This acceptance may involve approval of detached service on the part of a small, rotating cadre of faculty members to fulfill institutional commitments. While many of the problems outlined arise in such arrangements, the best approach to a workable compromise appears to be to consider the faculty members affected to be "on duty abroad" and not on personal leave in the usual sense. The faculty member is cooperating in a worthwhile *institutional* endeavor.

Not all opportunities which involve conflict of mission require absence on the part of the teacher-scholar from the academic community. One of the most difficult lines to draw is that in respect to a research enterprise established in the immediate neighborhood of the university either for profit or for national security or other worthy purposes. Since a university has no precise means of measuring the time or effort of its members, it must depend upon the acceptance of one's obligations as a faculty member by each individual. Close proximity encourages excessive diversion of energies which a considerable distance would make clear. Further, leadership in a parallel enterprise develops subtle temptations to employ junior teacher-scholars at salaries more generous than the university can provide and in research activities which may be more beneficial to a sponsor than to a scholar's career.

To meet this special problem, it appears justifiable to supplement the general policy already suggested by a provision that no member of the university faculty on regular appointment should become a responsible executive officer of an established, ongoing research enterprise which carries on research in the professor's own field. It is difficult to be a responsible officer in two parallel enterprises, especially in the same community, without facing conflicts of interest. This does not foreclose an arrangement negotiated by outside principals for a reasonable amount of consultation by the professor, provided it falls within the terms earlier outlined. But the professor is a part of management in the university, and he should not become a part of another management which seeks his services or those of his colleagues in university management or of the students entrusted to their care.

Another outside activity which appeals to some faculty members is participation in local politics and seeking election to a local, part-time political office. This is best interpreted as an activity entered upon by the professor as a citizen and involving his free time apart from his academic duties. Only when election to office involves protracted absence from the campus or considerable diversion of energies must the university ask the member to request leave of absence or, in the limiting case, to alter his career. It is not alone a matter of persistent preoccupation with external affairs, but also of the difficulty of preserving the intellectual independence of the academic scholar when he must adapt himself to the pressures of political expediency.

A similar problem arises when a professor shifts his main interest to political journalism or to popular programs on television or the lecture circuit. If the university has become a home base for activities in which high remuneration for skilled performance dulls the appeal of thorough teaching and critical scholarship, the professor has ceased to be a teacher-scholar as the term is here employed. At some appropriate time, he should be asked to decide which career he prefers. Again, service to society does not require the university to become a livery stable for popular talent.

In concluding this consideration of the role of the university and its faculty as a critical source of new knowledge, ideas, and value judgments in the society of which it is a part, it must be emphasized that much depends upon the traditions of service which subtly permeate the climate of the particular institution. The participation of members of a faculty in activities of national concern is bound to encourage interest on the part of students in matters of national concern. This, in turn, influences their attitude in future years in their own activity beyond that of earning a living. If, however, the interest of a faculty member is mainly in outside endeavors which add to his income at the expense of time and effort in teaching, the students have a right to take a dim view of the matter. The best posture a university can attain in relation to the activity of its faculty in the outside world is that which results from a response to an established tradition of public service balanced by a concern for excellence of performance *within* the university. Clearly stated and intelligently administered policies will help, but the best control is that of well-accepted assumptions. These develop as a reflection of the example of dedicated men, past and present, who in their careers have merged teaching, scholarship, and service to society in a mutually reinforcing pattern.

5

CONTINUING
EDUCATION
AND MID-CAREER
PROGRAMS

The service of the university in the communication of knowledge, ideas, and value judgments to those outside the academic world does not need to be confined to that growing out of the individual initiative of its faculty. The institution, as such, has the choice of whether to confine its instruction to full-time, degree candidates or to enter into (*a*) programs of part-time, continuing education for adults or (*b*) mid-career programs for practitioners in the various professions. The publicly supported university today has little choice but to expand the scope of its instructional activities in many directions. The private university, especially that in the tradition of the liberal university of limited size, still has a choice of whether to expand at all and in what way. Several considerations are involved in a wise decision on how best to utilize the faculty talent and energies, the administrative capacity, and the facilities which may be available for other than the main mission of the university. It is likely that a private liberal university will find that the most effective way it can extend its educational mission is through mid-career programs for practitioners in the various professions.

There is much reason to believe that a private, liberal university which has become highly selective in both faculty development and student admissions is not well adapted to become the sponsor of programs for part-time, continuing, general education for adults. Such extension programs can seldom be sufficiently selective in enrollments to permit a level or method of instruction comparable to that in advanced undergraduate or graduate courses in the regular curriculum of the university. Since many adult enrollees are returning to formal study after some time span beyond their college or high school years, most courses offered are likely to be elementary in content and deliberate in pacing. Necessary economies usually require heavy use of the lecture method and of readily available materials chosen to sustain interest. The professor who is especially effective in underclass instruction may be able to adapt himself readily to the kind of teaching needed, but many other members of a faculty find that a drastic shift of gears becomes necessary to suit the expectations of the older person seeking a limited acquaintance with a demanding discipline.

Since a highly qualified faculty of teacher-scholars is a most precious resource in a liberal university, it is questionable whether such a faculty should be diverted to a type of teaching or to assisting a kind of student for which it is not best suited. The contribution of a widespread development of extension courses for adults to a democratic society is by no means discounted, but the choice of instruments to provide such courses should reflect the highest comparative advantage in the use of scarce resources.

The diversion of the time and energies of the normally appointed teacher-scholar to adult, general education might be avoided by employing a sufficient number of additional teachers, part-time or full-time, for this specific purpose. This, however, involves many sticky problems. How are such adjunct teachers to be selected, and by whom? What is their status in terms of salary, rank, tenure, voting privileges, and rights of participation in departmental and university activities? Are they to be "second-class citizens" in the academic community? How are the courses given in extension programs to be controlled in level, quality, or performance required? Can degrees be earned in such programs, and, if so, how are they to be equated with those in regular programs?

Apart from these special problems in administering extension programs parallel with its normal mission, a liberal university of the type here concerned creates for itself an additional difficulty, as previously discussed, in properly utilizing the time and effort of its regular faculty. If professors on regular appointment teach in elementary extension courses, they are not, in most cases, being used to their highest advantage. If they so teach apart from their normal schedules and for additional compensation, the university is encouraging "moonlighting" of a sort which seldom adds to a professor's growth in his discipline. Yet those in charge of extension programs may find it much easier to recruit faculty already on campus than to seek elsewhere, even though the salary rate per course may be well below any estimated equivalent in the normal degree programs of the university.

Many universities, especially in urban centers, find extension, general-education programs a source of public support and considerable financial advantage to both the institution and the faculty employed. However, it is a considered judgment based on long experience that a private, liberal university with a carefully selected faculty and student body in its normal programs does well to leave the development of general, adult education to the public-supported institutions which can more readily adjust themselves to this type of auxiliary enterprise. The policy of abstaining from extension activities is sometimes a basis for the criticism that the university does not recognize its obligations to its local community. But the "community" of a liberal university is the nation, now and in the long future. Its best ally in softening such criticism is a vigorous and effective state university with a well-developed network of extension centers.

Distinct from programs of continuing, general education for adults are those specifically designed to provide postgraduate, professionally oriented courses for selected persons in mid-career. In these latter programs, the emphasis shifts from supplementing the cultural development or elementary skills of the adult student to enhancing the capacity of the fully trained, professional specialist by intensive work in the newer developments in his field. Here, the university faculty can use the best of its talents in interactive education through the means of new knowledge, new ideas, and well-developed value judgments. Further, the practical experience of the mid-career specialist acts as a balancing element to the more theoretical approach of the professor. Instead of the faculty member going out into the world of affairs or industry, the mature practitioner brings his evidence and judgments to the graduate seminar on campus. The fresh evidence and even the practical hunches introduced into discussions enliven the educational process for all participants. Much of the practitioner's concern for relevancy rubs off on the teacher as well as on other students who are less acquainted with the work of the world.

An important by-product of the interaction of the teacher-scholar with the mature practitioner in an associated field is the lessening of any rigidification of concepts and approaches by both of them. The professor, accustomed to respectful students seeking a degree, may come to overvalue exact and systematic logic in areas where many imponderables require intuition and judgment as well. The practitioner, on his part, may overvalue "practical" judgment at the expense of intensive, logical analysis on the basis of tested principles. Each gains by the interaction of minds and is encouraged to broaden his approach in seeking truth.

Mid-career programs for selected groups of professional or administrative personnel can take many forms. The simplest to organize are summer institutes of limited duration which emphasize the newer developments in a discipline or area of policy, whether for teachers, research scholars, or administrators. In planning such institutes, the particular strengths of the university in faculty and other resources can be drawn upon to provide a core group of professors who will take leadership in planning the educational content of the sessions. Ideally, the housekeeping preparations for such institutes should not fall on faculty members. Again, the latter should be used to their highest advantage in interactive education in the frontiers of their field. While the discussion of new knowledge, new problems, and new research techniques is the normal activity in these institutes, new methods of instruction, as in mathematics and language, are appropriate subjects in helping experienced teachers to adjust to change.

A more demanding type of program for mid-career practitioners is the year-long course for governmental and other executives selected for their exceptional potential. A flow of candidates for such programs involves a degree of sophistication and foresight which only the federal government and a few large corporations have yet attained. The curriculum of the program requires most careful planning by a responsible faculty committee. While some existing graduate courses may fit the need of seasoned executives, others must be developed which will provide a stimulating interplay between analysis and policy.

Despite a heavy investment by employers, enrollees, faculty, and the university, the returns on such mid-career programs appear to justify steadily increasing development. It is here that the liberal university can cooperate in improving the leadership of the state and the corporation with the greatest certainty that both faculty use and student potential are at a level of high comparative advantage. Further, the liberal university has a special contribution to make in such programs because of its emphasis upon fundamental and integrated approaches to ideas and values. The mature executive does not come to the university to sharpen his technical skills but to enrich his understanding and judgment in determining the complex issues facing public and corporate leaders today.

The time may come when lawyers, architects, engineers, and other professional men faced with the problems of an urban, industrial society may become candidates for intensive, year-long mid-career programs. The medical profession appears to favor more specialized training in new diagnostic or surgical techniques, but the professions which are engaged in developing and implementing public policy can no longer take a narrow view of the elements which affect that policy. The liberal university, especially, should stand ready to assist the leaders of these professions when methods are developed to permit selected mid-career members to return to the university. The university for its part should maintain high standards of admission and intellectual content. The professions have a right to ask that the courses be adjusted to the maturity and experience of those enrolled and that they be taught by faculty members of exceptional insight and breadth of understanding. With this development, the liberal university, as an institution, would enlarge its service to its society and time far more effectively than by competing with the great, publicly financed institutions in widespread systems of part-time general or technical adult education.

6

THE
ROLE OF
THE UNIVERSITY
PRESS

The traditional vehicle of the scholar in communicating his findings and judgments to all who may be interested is the printed page. The publication of specialized books and learned journals has become so essential in the mutual reinforcement of scholarly research and its contribution to intellectual progress that it is an appropriate activity of a university. The commercial press has provided a wide range of books and periodicals for all kinds of readers. However, it is evident that the requirement that publishing ventures must, on average, pay their way limits the degree to which scholarly books of limited circulation can be produced commercially. Under these conditions, it has become the mission of the university press to make sure that scholarly results of true worth and reasonable significance are not wasted because their publication is not profitable in commerical terms.

The university has several advantages in entering the demanding business of scholarly publication. It also faces several hazards. A primary advantage is the presence of teacher-scholars who, discipline by discipline, must be cognizant of the literature in their special field and able to evaluate the proffered contributions of fellow scholars with insight and authority. Further, they should be able to advise an author, through the editorial staff of the university press, how a manuscript can be improved in order that it may take its proper place in the body of evolving scholarship in the field.

Of value to the university itself is the fact that faculty participation in the activity of a university press sharpens the abilities of the teacher-scholar in the demanding art of developing a book of excellence which embodies lucidity, interest, precision, and style, no matter what the field. Just as the effective teacher must come to sense the response of the student, so the effective publisher and those who advise him must understand the probable response of readers. In cooperating with an associated university press, the professor-critic gains experience in an area of intercommunication which will serve him well in his own writing and teaching.

Another advantage of a university press to both the university and the faculty member is that the press can give special attention to fields of unusual strength in the university, and especially those pushing out new frontiers of learning and discovery. Not only is the faculty group concerned with the particular field an invaluable source of editorial support, but, also, it becomes a means of searching out potential authors. The development of a series of excellent publications in a field of strength not only helps to enliven that area of scholarship within the university, but enhances throughout the country and the world the recognition of the standing of the department and the total university. Universities are bound to vary in the relative strength of the many disciplines they cover. A flow of distinguished books, whether by local authors or others, does much to reinforce, over time, the particular areas of excellence which give tone to the total institution.

Bookmaking in the physical sense is an appropriate area of interest for teacher-scholars and the university. As a centuries-old art, printing has long been intimately involved in the progress of learning and the enjoyment of scholarship. A university press should be as proud of the form of its books as of their content. The cultivation of taste for fine printing, binding, and general format, adapted to content and readership, is itself a means of enhancing the intellectual and esthetic satisfactions of the author, the publisher, and the reader. Attractive books, as well as other university publications, are an appropriate support to the total effort of a university to improve the sense of style on the part of all those who make up an academic community.

There are also hazards in the development of a first-class university press. Among these is the danger that the press may become too responsive to the interests of the faculty and administration of the associated university at the expense of standards in determining which books it will publish or what services it will perform. The general board and editorial board of a university press should develop a large degree of autonomy for the long-run interest of all concerned. The standards of quality of publications should be correlated with national standards established by the best presses and the best scholars. The decisions of an editorial board should be based in large measure upon the evaluations of outside readers and not alone upon those of the colleagues of a local author.

In order to establish standards and to provide a well-balanced list of publications, a university press should seek to find authors throughout the country who can best fit its programs of publication, even though most programs have been initiated to reflect local interests and strengths. The inclusion of authors from other universities or from outside academia not only strengthens the list, but places local authors on a demanding competitive basis in terms of both scholarship and the presentation of their material. In this way the press becomes a supplementary stimulus in enhancing the quality of scholarship and writing within the university. This policy requires, of course, a degree of impartiality on the part of the director of the press, his editors, and the associated faculty editorial board which must be firmly supported by the senior administration of the university. Fortunately, the test of reviews in scholarly and other journals, as well as sales related to prospective market, soon indicates whether judgments have been parochial.

An unfortunate early use of the university press was the publication of doctoral theses presented within the sponsoring university. While hundreds of doctoral theses have grown into books of quality and significance, the decision of a university press must relate to a book as such and to a worldwide market, not to the worthiness of a candidate's first efforts in scholarly writing to justify a Ph.D. degree. Nothing will reduce the effectiveness of a university press more drastically than to become known as the publisher of doctoral theses. Not only is the opportunity to build a balanced and distinguished list curtailed, but the function of the press as a stimulus to mature scholarship on the part of the faculty is dulled. This does not prevent the press from encouraging young scholars to develop a book worthy of publication growing out of interests, ideas, and material related to one's thesis. But this may take years of additional independent work on the part of the author in order to lift the quality of the product to that which can hold its own before the world of scholarship.

Another hazard for the university press is the pressure from faculty groups to publish the papers given at conferences held on campus. The persuasive effort becomes acute when some distinguished local scholar is to be honored by a *Festschrift*. The safest rule to follow appears to be, again, that the quality and mutual reinforcement of the combined manuscripts must make a scholarly book of sufficient significance to warrant publication regardless of parochial concerns. Rather than relying on faculty initiative alone, the editors of a university press, who come to know the scholarly work of individual professors on a campus, can help them to focus their efforts on useful, well-integrated publications. Since both the staff of the press and the members of the faculty have the support of continuing, affiliated institutions, they can join in planning scholarly projects of long duration without the uncertainties of commercial arrangements.

The most difficult question faced by the university press is one of economic judgment: should a book of unquestioned scholarship, but of exceptionally limited readership, be published? Even with complete subsidization of costs, there is a minimum use in terms of copies sold or otherwise distributed below which publication of a manuscript appears to be unjustified. The normal distribution of scholarly books will range well under that required for commercial publication. The university press must serve some fields of scholarship which require heavy subsidization from the time of initial investigation to finished publication. But there remains the issue of sound economy in balancing the relative costs of *printed* publication against readership. While every scholar gains deep satisfaction from a handsome book bearing his name, rising costs may require, on occasion, the use of modern substitutes for conventional printing and binding in disseminating his contributions.

The problems for the university in its relations with its press are those of legal control and of the degree and methods of subsidization. The simplest arrangement is that to make the press a regular department of the university and determine an appropriate allocation for it in the general budget each year. This may avoid tax problems and afford a degree of flexibility, especially in a university which is anxious to enlarge rapidly the activities of its press. It is true, however, that much is gained by a larger degree of autonomy within the press and with it a sense of self-reliant enterprise in building its own reputation as an affiliated but separate organization.

Book publishing remains one of the few business activities where every product is a unique item and where success in both qualitative and financial terms grows out of a long series of independent but consistent decisions. No matter how much helpful advice the editorial staff of the press may obtain from a university faculty and from outside scholars, the management of the press should make its own decisions to a much greater degree than a teaching department within a general faculty or a library or a computing center does. The making of distinguished books requires closely interlocking teamwork from the development of a flow of manuscripts, through editing, design, and production, to the intelligent cultivation of readership. These conditions appear to justify the organization of the press as a distinct corporate body in terms of legal, financial, and executive responsibility with university participation effected through a board of directors with adequate university representation. As a means of assuring high scholarly standards, an editorial committee of the board, made up of professors appointed by the president of the university, can be required to review and approve each book before publication. An advantage of such a separate board is that some members can be persons from outside the university with long experience in publishing, finance, and the law.

Legal separation of the press from the university does not relieve the university of the financial obligation of undergirding, to a reasonable degree, an important adjunct to its total mission. Such support can be given through the provision of space, services, or assistance in developing outside grants; through general grants; or through the development of departmental publication funds. As with all other areas of university activity, the maintenance of excellence in scholarly publishing and the freedom to push the frontiers of learning in depth and breadth are more important than precisely balancing costs. A university press, as a separate business enterprise, must learn to live within its means, year by year; but as a closely affiliated participant in the scholarly life of the university it needs to grow in strength as the university develops new fields of instruction and scholarship. Since it cannot sell stock or rely on profits alone, it must have help, when needed, from the parent institution to assure both excellence and growth. A distinguished university press, on its part, becomes known throughout the scholarly world and enhances the achievement and the recognition of the university in all aspects of its mission.

PROBLEMS
OF
ECONOMY
AND
CONTROL

1

THE OPTIMAL SIZE OF ENROLLMENT

It is a well-tested premise in the analysis of human organizations that the size of an organization should be related to its major function. Further, those human organizations in which direct and informal interpersonal relations are a paramount pattern and purpose have been found to be most viable and effective when the size of the principal, significant unit is relatively small. As interpersonal relations become more formalized and hierarchical layers develop, an organization may expand in size with but limited loss in effectiveness; but with larger size the concept of command, whether by personal direction or established rules, begins to gain relatively greater importance than individual response.

A farm or a country store in years long past depended largely in its organizational effectiveness upon close interpersonal relations and response. A steel mill or automobile assembly plant must, for the sake of efficiency, embody a whole system of command elements in the form of rules, standard practices, and hierarchical authorities at various levels. In fact, the problem of modern industrial relations in large enterprises has been to insure that valuable elements of employee response have not become lost in the proliferation of controls. Size itself makes response and the close interpersonal relations which nurture response more difficult to assure.

This brief and much simplified reference to organizational analysis has much relevance to the determination of the optimum size of a university and, particularly, a liberal university. True *education*, to be effective, is an interactive process between teacher and taught, and between student and fellow student. *Training* to conform to a predetermined skill or conclusion can be carried on with larger groups. The technique, fact, or conclusion can be transmitted by word of mouth, by the printed page, by graphic illustration, or by electronic gear of many kinds. A more or less spotty response can be gained by testing, but it is essentially a testing of conformity unless the teacher does more than grade the papers.

There is much need for training in skills and for education in conformity, as in the use of standard procedures in language and mathematics. Even the facts of history and geography are a proper part of elementary and secondary education. But the one-way transmission of established data, even with testing to assure individual "reception," should give way to *interactive* education, with constant, individualized response, as the student moves up through the university. This is of the highest importance in a *liberal* university, which seeks to enhance understanding and sensitivity in respect to values, principles, judgments, and insights. In the liberal university, interactive, individualized response is the pattern of life for the student, the faculty member, and those who must sustain an enveloping condition of good order.

The size of an organization affects the degree to which response can be direct, informal, and free, as opposed to a condition where elements of command and conformity become enlarged through rules, required procedures, and one-way transmission of approved knowledge. Because of this, the size of a liberal university is of significance. It is true that a large institution may strive to offset the pressures toward command and conformity by creating many subdivisions of small size and relative independence. But so long as these subdivisions must conform by rule or practice to organizationwide standards in certain attributes, such as costs, teacher-student ratios, instructional methods, and student life, it is difficult to assure the degree of diversity and freedom which a pervasive climate of individualized response requires. It may be possible to attenuate the influence of institutional size upon the climate of interactive response in the day-to-day educational process, but it is more likely in large institutions that student response will find its outlet increasingly through extracurricular channels such as social, cultural, and political organization and activity, and in sports, whether as participant or observer.

It is also true that the interactive, individualized education which emphasizes response is expensive. This is especially true now that college and university professors are gaining an economic status more comparable to that of professional men and even business executives of similar quality. Further, such education now requires libraries, laboratories, and other facilities of burgeoning cost. Apart from factors affecting human organization and optimum size related to response, economic factors militate against increasing size in liberal universities. Since human quality and family resources are not closely correlated, the heavy cost of liberal education, as here defined, cannot be properly borne by full-cost tuition charges. Nor is the state likely to finance the full cost for greatly increased numbers. The economics of liberal education of high quality appears, therefore, to encourage those institutions which consider such education as their traditional mission to control size rigorously, even at the expense of increasingly selective admissions procedures.

The problem of optimum size of the institution in liberal education is not a recent development, but the rapidly growing demand for higher education has now made it acute. A century or more of proliferation of small, independent colleges now seems to be a phase of educational history that cannot be repeated in the face of sharply rising costs and restricted income sources. Through ever-widening and deepening channels, the flow of funds for higher education has been diverted to large-scale public programs. Even in those private colleges with a long tradition of liberal education, there are strong pressures to enlarge, in order to attract both superior students and larger funds in a time when graduate education and the coverage of new fields seem to be necessary for high visibility. The older private universities of liberal tradition are being subjected to pressure not only to admit more students, but to expand coverage in many expensive ways. The issue of size has, indeed, become acute.

How can a liberal university grow in size without facing the hazards which size brings? Perhaps there is no way, but many are being tried. One way that has been used is to break up the university into a system of relatively small residential colleges. So far as student life becomes centered in such colleges, considerable gain is made. But the problems of assuring individual, interactive response in the instructional operations of the university, despite large overall size, remain. This can be solved only by a parallel extension of small-group or individualized instruction, which is very expensive. While some economies in administration and some advantages in the use of specialized faculty talent can be gained by this means, there are still problems concerning total size which are very troublesome.

A central problem for a university which has broken up its student body into smaller residential colleges, even with a high investment in faculty for interactive instruction, is that of leadership and common personality. Academic leadership in both the university and the teaching departments requires sustained and sensitive intercommunication and the acceptance of common traditions and objectives. The more the units of the total university become separate in order to avoid the influences of large size, the more likely will be the emergence of diverse loci of leadership and of conflicting emphases in policy, standards, and objectives. This is particularly true if the separate subdivisions come to favor diverse approaches to learning, such as science over the humanities, or preprofessional education over fundamental studies. It does not require the formal division into administrative schools to encourage specialization in outlook. An old and strong liberal institution can sustain the tradition of a single personality, supported by a vigorous integrating leadership in the university as a whole. But in less favorable circumstances, new ventures in the "multiple-college" or "cluster-college" approach face conflicting pressures which are difficult to resolve.

The existence of a common budget introduces a problem for the multiple-college university when instruction as well as residential arrangements is decentralized. Differentiated instructional programs, whether by method or subject, leads to sizable differences in cost. If all units are kept on a par in costs per student, the influence of size creeps in. It is most difficult for the central leadership of the university to explain away differences in financial support to the subdivision that is getting less than another comparable subdivision.

The multiple-college plan also creates problems in faculty development. How far should the procedures for the appointment and advancement of a professor teaching in a particular college be influenced by his colleagues in that college, regardless of discipline, as distinguished from those in his discipline throughout the university? His close colleagues within the college are concerned with his effectiveness as a teacher and his responsible participation in the life of the smaller unit. Those in his discipline in the university are concerned with his scholarship in his special subfield and with whether he helps to give balance and distinction to a university-wide department offering graduate instruction and promoting research. Procedures can be developed to bring all points of view to bear, but the existence of countervailing tensions in the professor and the institution cannot be ignored. It would be unfortunate if the inadequate resolution of the problem should lead to two categories of professors, those who concentrate their interests and gain advancement by undergraduate teaching in a subordinate college and those who enjoy preferred status as "university" professors giving graduate instruction and carrying on research. This may be the outcome—one that would reduce the multiple-college system to a holding-company operation over colleges that, except for financial support from a jealous parent, might do better on their own.

It appears that these and other forces at work in a university which seeks to offset large size by the multiple-college approach tend to bring the university to the situation which some large state universities have long accepted. With size there must be a hierarchical structure, with elaborate subdivision of responsibility and a strong central control through the budgetary process. Schools become specialized and leadership diffused. As suggested early in this chapter, this is the way many types of large-scale operations can be administered and a large volume of service rendered. But in terms of the liberal university here discussed, size has then been mastered by a change in both style and mission in the educational process. The liberal university has become the "multiversity," unless the blessings of age, liberal tradition, and strong leadership have overcome the subtle and persistent influences of size on the nature and functioning of a human organization and on the character of the educational process which that organization can best provide.

Apart from the influences of size on the character of the educational process and on the nature of university organization which have been discussed, it is evident that many larger universities have developed effective countermeasures to reduce the impact of increasing size upon the way of life of the individual student. Residential arrangements have been rapidly expanded and have been planned to encourage the formation of congenial subcommunities. Carefully designed student unions have become attractive centers for a wide range of social and cultural activities. Intercollegiate games in a wide variety of sports, lecture and musical programs, traditional celebrations, and a host of student activities have created a friendly and stimulating climate within the university community. The American problem of size has been countered by the American genius for organization. This may be the solution in many spheres of American life, but in higher education it does more to provide for the social and cultural maturation of the student than to substitute for the development of his intellectual powers through close interaction with demanding teacher-scholars.

The countermeasures taken by the large multiversity to overcome the problems of size in the educational process include a wide range of devices, including closed-circuit television, language laboratories, programmed instruction, visual aids, and computers. While these are valuable supporting mechanisms in many aspects of instruction in an electronic age, they fall short of providing an effective substitute for the kind of educational process which is the central concern of the liberal university.

Despite a sustained conviction that increasing size and enrollments create changes in institutional character and in the ability to provide a climate of informal, interactive education, liberal universities today face two persistent pressures toward growth which are most difficult to withstand. First is the urge to add new fields of coverage which grow out of or reinforce existing fields. Examples include the desire to extend instruction in linguistics as a base for the study of a wide spectrum of languages. Area programs require more depth in the total culture and history of expanding regions of interest. In science, biochemistry, solid-state physics, and plasma physics have become essential extensions of older fields. In engineering, the rapid development of electronics and computer technology, even at the fundamental level of applied science, strongly encourages the expansion of the curriculum. A discussion of the university policies involved will come later, but the evident consequence of these and many other new coverages, unless older coverages are vigorously pruned, is that more students must be enrolled to utilize the additional instructional capacity involved, if older programs are not to be depopulated. If older programs have been manned properly, to spread the same number of students over a broader curriculum leads to underutilization of costly faculty time, an increase in an already expensive ratio of teachers to students and a loss of opportunity to help more students obtain a liberal education. There is no assurance that additional enrollments will neatly balance the new capacity created through extended subject coverage. But it is evident that an expansion of faculty without an increase of students makes instruction per student more costly. Old coverages have a way of persisting, not only because they are often needed, but, even if they are of declining relevance, because those who teach them may be years short of retirement.

A second pressure upon liberal universities is to provide an increasing flow of university-level teachers for an expanding national program of higher education. Even though tight control is exercised upon undergraduate enrollments, it is difficult to withstand the argument that distinguished liberal universities should provide a larger flow of "seed corn" to strengthen the quality of university faculties throughout the country. Without question, larger graduate enrollments and seminars do affect the character and quality of instruction in terms of interactive education. The size of graduate enrollments also affects student life and the climate of administration. Fortunately, graduate admissions can be related to departmental capacity and to subject coverage. But even with this advantage, the total effect of increasing size involves the basic problems earlier discussed.

Caught in the pressures for increasing enrollments, the liberal university must seek to respond sufficiently to the needs of its society without impairing its total, long-run contribution. It must remain true to its own style of education and sustain the conviction that this is *its* best way to serve a pluralistic society which has room for many styles. Falling between the large number of small colleges of the kind from which it developed and the vast public multiversities, it must insist upon those conditions of life which give it the opportunity to invest heavily in individual students and individual teacher-scholars who give promise of high returns. The liberal university of moderate size must ask that it be judged by its impact on society past, present, and future, rather than on the number of students it enrolls or the areas of learning it covers. It must in its mission counter the pressures for bigness in American life in order to concentrate its efforts on providing those resources of men and ideas which it believes it can better produce without the assumed economies of size. In following this policy, it respects a long-tested principle in human organization—that size should be related to function.

THE
CONTROL
OF SUBJECT
COVERAGE
AND
SPECIALIZATION

At no point in the administrative operations of a university are countervailing tensions more evident than in the determination of the subjects to be covered and the degree of specialization within each subject. The forces toward differentiation and specialization are ever present. They arise out of the natural urge of the teacher-scholar with academic freedom to pursue his chosen field in increasing depth and into newly discovered frontiers of knowledge. What he learns at the cutting edge of his scholarship and research he is likely to want to teach, at least in part. To retreat to older or more general subject matter in his courses, because this is necessary for more elementary instruction, requires a shift from the excitement of the frontier to the increasing tedium of familiar paths. Yet the faculty member who feels the urge toward specialization at the edges of learning is a part of the management of the department and of the university which must determine the character and bounds of the curriculum. The shift from individual interest to corporate responsibility in determining curricular policy is not easy, and some members never make it.

Yet the forces toward integration in a liberal university must be fully able to counterbalance those toward differentiation, if the institution is to fulfill its proper role. For the liberal university, institutional integrity is essential. These forces must arise from strong leadership at the center, supported by effective organization, communications, and procedures, and implemented by understanding cooperation by the senior leadership of schools and departments. It is here that tradition, the projection of past leadership, is an important resource. It is far easier to restrain proliferation of courses if it is generally *assumed* that restraint is a virtue.

To realize that restraint is not the highest virtue in American academic planning requires but a scanning of the catalogues of a dozen universities picked at random. In some, the proliferation of courses is overwhelming. The example of seventy-two courses in educational psychology in one large university can be duplicated all too often. The listing of courses on individual authors in literature or on special approaches to higher mathematics fills pages of closely printed text. The explosion of knowledge may fill libraries, but this is far less expensive than its effect in the offering of hundreds of additional courses for which teachers, staff support, and space must be provided.

Whatever the economic consequences of subject differentiation and course proliferation in university administration, the educational consequences are more distressing. Breaking up learning into small bits and pieces in the structuring of the curriculum strongly suggests that the dispensing of knowledge, rather than the education of the student, has come to be the role of the teacher. Yet, it must be repeated, knowledge should be the *means* of education, not its end. It does not follow that the newest bit of knowledge gained by the teacher in his own research is the best means of enlarging the mind of the student or of enhancing his intellectual potential and sense of values. A third-class poem or a forgotten general may be a worthy subject for an article in a learned journal, but as the stimuli of lively, interactive discussion in a class or seminar they leave much to be desired. The result of the professor's urge to transmit his newfound material to his students is often a dull, pedestrian parade of erudition passively recorded in notebooks. Only the most brilliant teachers can project a view of the world through a keyhole, and they are usually wise enough to open the door in order that the student may catch a wider view.

A policy of restraint against the proliferation of courses and specialized subject matter in a curriculum is, therefore, essentially an *educational* policy. It may have wholesome economic effects as well, but these do not necessarily follow if restraint in determining the number of courses permits greater use of teaching manpower in each course given, with more opportunity for interactive education. It may be argued that offering more courses leads to smaller courses in terms of class enrollments, but the reduction in size of class is then gained by accepting a questionable concept of education. Further, the proliferation of small courses creates problems in the efficient use of manpower, since it adds complexities and risks in planning teaching assignments as elections fluctuate and faculty specialization fails to match student preferences.

The soundest principle to follow in building a universitywide curriculum in a liberal institution is to move from the fundamental core of knowledge in each major discipline only so far as it is *educationally* necessary to do so. The test at each step is not what the individual professor wants to teach. It is, rather, what each department, acting as the corporate body charged with responsibility for the education of students in its discipline, believes to be the best body of knowledge to be used as a means of education. The department should have its restraining judgment reinforced by a central faculty committee representing other disciplines as well, so that the desire to please old friends or exaggerated notions of the importance of a discipline are tempered. The central faculty committee should be chaired by a senior officer who is by status protected from the temptation to participate in easy mutual accommodation and is fully cognizant of institutional educational traditions and of an institutional need for economy.

A senior academic officer who chairs a faculty committee on curriculum needs to develop the intuition and judgment of a middle linebacker in professional football if he is to control the pressures for course proliferation. Neither he nor his committee can comprehend the subject matter of a wide range of disciplines, but he can bring to the committee a body of relevant information such as statistical trends in course offerings and elections in any department seeking to expand its offerings; the courses of small election already offered; the teaching manpower available; the apparent duplications within and between departments; the balance of offerings by student level; and the arguments used for past additions. The chairman should help the committee in finding out, on appearance of a departmental representative, the true reason for the department's recommendation—whether it is a general conviction of need for a balanced program or a willingness to placate a restless or ambitious individual. Comparisons of offerings at other institutions may help in a few cases, but tight control is exceptional.

In addition to all the educational arguments he feels revelant, a senior academic officer has an entire right to explain the economic results of unwise expansion of course offerings and the possible diversion of funds otherwise available for uses of greater concern to the faculty. The academic administrator is often in a somewhat lonely position in holding to a rigorous policy. His best hope is to educate his committee and the chairmen of departments in the overall need for sound economy in both educational and financial terms.

The goal of curricular policy is, in sum, to assure that educational decisions do not become the by-product of the scholarly specialization of the faculty but, persistently, remain a reflection of the needs of the student. In a liberal university, the central place of the undergraduate college helps to make the needs of students more clearly evident. The principle that fundamental knowledge is a more appropriate means of education than the detailed products of personal scholarship is hard to deny in the lower and middle levels of instruction. The policy becomes more difficult to assure, however, in upper-level and graduate courses. But in relative terms, even greater restraint is required as the professor increasingly sees the student in his own image and unconsciously assumes that he should be enthused by the same analysis of the twigs of learning which excite the professor, rather than needing help in understanding the branches from which many twigs will grow.

The policy of restraint in the proliferation of courses here advanced would become more trying to the spirit of many teacher-scholars if there were not means of introducing elements of specialization within the general educational process. Just as the teacher-scholar wants to analyze a problem in depth or to search out some new frontier, so does the more able student. The change in gear from fundamental learning to specialized analysis can be provided through independent work in the upper-class years and in the protracted labors on the doctoral thesis. Here "independence" permits individual choice of subject, which is usually far more specialized than that given much attention in a general course. As many professors and institutions have learned, "independence" does not mean reduced faculty effort in interactive education. The subjects chosen by students may not always parallel some professor's research interest, but there is a likelihood that many will; wise assignment can help satisfy the desire of each professor to lead some students, at least, nearer to his chosen frontier.

Another means of adjusting the balance between curricular restraint and freedom of experimentation is the special, one-time seminar. A limited number of such seminars, authorized annually after careful evaluation of their interest and relevancy, can be offered to highly qualified undergraduates. They should be kept distinct from graduate seminars for professionally oriented students, since their aim is more to challenge the generalist than to prepare the specialist. Further, they should not be repeated, lest they become courses. Since there are usually a number of undergraduates who are more stimulating than many graduate students, the professor who has been permitted to introduce such students to a somewhat more specialized consideration of a subject in his field of interest may return to his normal teaching with less concern about a general policy of restraint. The fact that such special, one-time seminars require much preparation and intensive teaching effort tends to control their proliferation. They provide, however, a degree of elasticity which is desirable in any enduring structure.

While restraint may epitomize the proper policy and tradition in the control of curricular growth, it still does not provide an easy answer to the specific questions which the academic administrator faces each year. Proposals for new programs and courses are supported by men of enthusiasm and persuasive powers. Every professor and every department has the right to believe that *their* contribution to understanding is of paramount importance. Older disciplines will emphasize institutional prestige and newer disciplines the rapidity of change, in attempting to convince the central administration that new courses must be added. A well-used argument is that brilliant younger professors cannot be retained unless they are given courses which permit them to enlarge upon the subject of their doctoral thesis or of their first book. It is suggested that some other university from which an offer is sure to come does not have such a rigid, old-fashioned notion that the curriculum should be closely integrated.

In the balancing of all pressures, it is evident that a curriculum must grow as knowledge and issues in our society become more extensive and complex. Perhaps the most useful analogy to be kept in mind in determining year-by-year policy is that of a great and growing tree. New branches and sub-branches should grow from strength, from the vital sap moving up from the roots, trunk, and main branches of a long-established organism. The effective pressures for change should come from within, from limbs already strong. While the tree must live in a world of sun, rain, and wind, it must grow in its own form, with balance and integrity. To shift the analogy, a liberal university is not a department store where each floor manager seeks to satisfy *his* particular customers. It is not a system of specialty shops leased out under a single roof. A liberal university is a very special kind of human organization which, like a tree, must grow in a way peculiar to itself and its own vital resources. The analogy of a growing tree suggests a general approach in curricular administration. This consists in asking any department that proposes a new course, as a standing requirement, to analyze all its existing courses and to indicate which course can be pruned away if a new course is deemed essential. Experience has shown that courses become obsolete, especially as faculty members age, resign, retire, or change their interests. New knowledge may be a better means of education than old knowledge, if both are sufficiently fundamental. By premising that any new course must, if possible, be offset by pruning out an old course, a department is strongly encouraged to review periodically its entire program of offerings. The emphasis upon departmental responsibility and a normal process of total review reinforces the concept of integrity and helps to overcome the resistance of members whose courses have lost their excitement and relevancy. Courses are an expression of personality, and the teacher involved is seldom the best judge of his own contribution. The central administration must reinforce introspective consideration by the department of the balance and vigor of a total program, even though it must also protect the dignity of the individual in other individual ways.

If a discipline has moved to new and important frontiers, or if a new discipline has evolved within the structure of the institution, a more significant decision must be made. It is probable that such a decision will involve one or more senior appointments to the faculty as well as the authorization of new courses. The creation of one new senior position involving salary, benefits, staff support, space, facilities, specialized library resources, and fellowship grants in a private university may well absorb the income from at least two million dollars of endowment. The economic consequences of a curricular decision to enter a new discipline or subdiscipline are, therefore, sufficient to give gravity to the decision.

The decision to enter a new discipline or a significant new area of coverage should involve the intensive participation of the related departments or school, the appropriate central committees on curriculum, both undergraduate and graduate, the senior academic officers, and, at the final stage, the full faculty. If, for example, a new department is to be created, the appropriate committee of the trustees should approve it at a time when consultation can assure that the new endeavor reflects the judgment of the trustees in relation to the total mission of the university and the best use of available resources. The president and his chief educational officers should act as the leaders in coordinating the process, once they are convinced of the soundness of the policy, even though the initiative and more specialized understanding of the new field come from the faculty. Resolving the issue of whether an important new venture in subject coverage is wise is a significant example of the mutual reinforcement of faculty, administration, and trustees in the effective governance of a liberal university.

Not all the hazards in determining a wise curricular policy arise from within. The policy makers in foundations and government agencies are not immune to the urge to indicate the areas that a university should cover, not in research alone, but in teaching oncoming generations. Their suggestions become more tempting if backed by funds, even though such funds are "developmental" and limited in period of availability. The external relations of a liberal university will be discussed later, but it is proper to register at this point the opinion that some of the more serious errors in curricular expansion in many universities have been made because some outside agency or well-financed individual encouraged the university to accept funds for an endeavor not appropriate to its self-determined mission. Foundations, governmental agencies, and well-intentioned individuals should be remembered in the grateful prayers of academic administrations for their munificent cooperation in financing internally determined growth, but their tempting suggestions to graft new limbs of *their* choosing on the growing curricular tree should receive the most cautious treatment. A university faculty and administration are far from omniscient in comprehending the needs of society, but they should know the traditions, mission, and alternative capabilities for curricular growth in *their* institution better than any outside agency.

An example of questionable anxiety to respond to outside suggestion in the building of curriculum is the multiplication of programs for area studies. As America took on increasing worldwide responsibilities after World War II, foundations and government agencies were quick to encourage universities to prepare students for service throughout the world. But area programs, fully developed, involve a wide range of language, cultural, historical, political, economic, and sociological disciplines. Further, they require scarce talent and expensive library support. While some weak attempts were made in coordinating the total scheme of university specialization, the availability of ready, yet insufficient, funds led many universities to duplicate the efforts of others to an extent unjustified by the overall needs of the country. It can be argued that the expansion of the horizons of the faculty and students of American universities has had a timely and wholesome effect, but the full consequences of any overexpansion of academic commitments at a time of financial stringency still lie ahead.

In a calm review of the forays of universities into multiple and duplicating area-study programs, it is now evident that a subtle error in policy was involved. In the excitement of incorporating new areas of *knowledge* into the curriculum, the fundamental truth that knowledge is but the means of education was discounted. Except for a very few professional career men, intensive work in any *specific* area of the world is not needed to understand the diversity of mankind and his institutions. A program of courses in one or two non-Western cultures, supported by courses in comparative institutions, can well serve most students in gaining the understanding they need. To offer a wide spectrum of area programs covering the far places of the world may please some professors and enhance institutional prestige, but it is a form of proliferation suggestive of seventy-two courses in educational psychology in another dimension. In the latter case, the educational psychologists were guilty of excessive zeal in narrow specialization. In the former, the university may have been unduly swayed by the tempting image of universality in its corporate knowledge of the world and its myriad cultures.

3

THE
CONTROL
OF THE USE
OF
TEACHING
MANPOWER

The most precious resource of a liberal university is a carefully selected, strongly motivated body of teacher-scholars which has, through years of development, come to match in balance and depth the curricular pattern of the university. Such a faculty is a more critical resource by far than the more obvious layout of structures, lecture halls, classrooms, and laboratories which impress the casual visitor and which often lead efficiency experts to propose round-the-year instruction in order to utilize available space. The intelligent use of space is, of course, a proper goal in academic administration, but the wise use of teaching manpower is of a much higher priority. Classrooms can be built in a year or two at a cost which can be measured in dollars. A strong and balanced faculty requires decades of farsighted planning, many favorable conditions, and sustained initiative to develop.

Unfortunately, in many universities the control of classroom use has been developed into a much more precise art than the control of teaching assignments or teaching hours. There has been some confusion in university administration between academic freedom to teach the truth as the professor sees it and the freedom of the professor to determine for himself how many hours he teaches, or in what courses, or to how many students. The former freedom must be jealously safeguarded. The latter freedom must be framed by the needs and resources of the institution, by an equitable pattern of mutual obligation, and by a close adjustment of the professional services to be rendered to the specific educational objective sought. With higher salaries and rapidly mounting supporting costs, the day of easygoing, casual assignment of teaching hours and of administrative ignorance of teaching costs, in all their complexity, is past.

In a leading university today, the cost of one teaching hour per academic year for a full professor may range from $2,500 to $5,000 for his salary and financial benefits alone. If the cost of paid leaves for scholarship is added, this is increased considerably. Office space, staff support, and facilities raise the figure to an impressive level. Obviously the planning and control of the use of a teaching hour multiplied by thousands is the key to sound educational economics. The more expensive higher education becomes, the more careful must be the use of critical resources. Fortunately, not all teacher-scholars are full professors, but the use of large numbers of junior and less costly personnel is bound to affect the quality of truly liberal, interactive education.

The planning, administration, and control of the use of faculty teaching hours in the modern university require an effective balance between departmental or school responsibility and universitywide responsibility. The department must be constantly aware of university policies and standards as it assigns hours to each course or to the many kinds of educational and administrative duties which are necessary in a complex instructional program. Such standards involve size of class or seminar, with minimum and maximum limits. They include norms in the use of various instructional methods, including advisory services in independent work at all levels, and also in allowances for administration and demanding committee assignments and in laboratory supervision. The chairman of the department and those who assist him in the allocation of teaching time should have sustained advice and support from the central administration in order to know when they are using critical resources wisely. Far greater cooperation and acceptance are gained if each department knows that its standards in the use of teaching hours are in accordance with general standards, subject to any reasonable adjustment which the nature of a particular discipline may require.

The establishment of general standards for teaching-hour assignments may be criticized by those who emphasize the difficulty of measuring the effort required in various kinds of teaching, such as in large lectures, small classes, or laboratory supervision. In practice, it is the chairman who balances the mix of assignments for each individual according to effort required. The central administration is concerned with costs, however, and needs some measure of the total duty time that is considered normal. Some science departments with a heavy load of laboratory supervision, graduate teaching, or supervision of research may develop norms distinct from those in "reading" departments, but the important factor is that for each area there shall be established, accepted standards which afford a basis for controlling instructional costs over time. To allow each department to assign expensive teaching hours without such standards leads to a drift toward looseness which few universities can afford.

But established standards in the use of teaching hours are not enough. Effective implementation requires both reporting and audit. As has already been discussed in dealing with academic administration, it is a sound practice to require a detailed report from each department, each term, on standard forms which indicate the assignment of hours by number for each professor and instructor, by course or other assigned duty. A summary of total hours assigned per course and enrollment per course is helpful. Only by the information in such a report can the chairman consolidate his knowledge of his own operations. Only by such reports can the deans of schools or the dean of the faculty be sure that standards are being implemented and that any proposed changes in assignment standards, teaching methods, departmental manning, or curricular offerings are justified.

Such close control of teaching-hour assignments may appear to some professors to be tainted with the odor of bureaucracy. They may overlook the evident fact that it is the sharp increase in their salaries and benefits, and in the costs of the supporting services they have come to expect, that makes orderly administration and control of the allocation of duty time so necessary. Despite every safeguard of academic freedom in teaching and scholarship, the professor still is a part of an economy where duty performed and compensation forthcoming form a single equation. A teaching salary is not a personal grant, subsidy, or pension. The trustees of the university are providing a flow of salary in exchange for a flow of service in an operation which must justify itself to all concerned in order to survive and flourish. The economics of the use of faculty manpower remains a segment of general economics even though a university sometimes seems to be a loosely organized partnership of independent professionals.

The by-products of close administration and control of teaching hours are many. While discussed more fully elsewhere in their administrative aspects, these by-products may be summarized to indicate their relevance to the problem of overall control. Analytical summaries will show significant trends, unaffected by fortuitous salary patterns or general changes in salary levels. Departmental costs for instruction can be separated from expenditures for staff support, facilities, or research activities. Information can be gained long before the financial office can prepare annual reports on departmental expenditures, and reasons for change can be more clearly diagnosed. Hour budgeting is more understandable to most chairmen than dollar budgeting, especially when individual salary levels, leaves, and turnover may be related to conditions beyond his control. Further, a chairman is much more impressed by the ratio of students taught per teaching hour in his department compared to that in a neighboring department than he is by gross dollar budgets covering dissimilar enrollments. These and many other advantages accrue from the term-by-term audit of the use of teaching manpower. The greatest overall gain is the sense of precision and equity which comes to be a part of the administrative climate. Exceptions and adjustments, which are so necessary in dealing with a wide range of disciplines and teaching situations, can be made knowingly and judiciously from general norms, rather than being permitted to develop with no more reason than ignorance, cozy tolerance, or parochial self-interest.

The effective administration of teaching assignments has become increasingly essential as universities take on more and more organized research projects. The time assigned to teaching should be a reciprocal of the time assigned to project research, given a normal total schedule. Government requirements in reporting the proportionate effort applied to contract research by each faculty member can be met without guesswork and without casual generosity on the part of an anxious professor seeking to reduce the charges to his contract by underestimating the time diverted from teaching. With precise time allocations in terms of normal teaching schedules, the total charges to instructional and one or more research accounts can be brought to balance total salary.

When adequate records on manpower utilization are available, many of the educational problems faced by the administration can be studied with some assurance that the economic consequences of proposed changes can be estimated in advance. For example, the introduction of a new program in area studies requiring one or more exotic languages and attracting but small enrollments can be weighed in terms of the teaching-hour requirements and the students taught per teaching hour in similar existing programs. The results of the study are likely to be useful in countering professorial enthusiasm. The degree of overload in teaching assignments, despite an under-enrollment in courses, in exotic languages is always a source of concern. There is a limit to the tolerance of the language specialist which, in time, creates pressure for additional manning.

In the past, when teaching hours were less costly in dollar terms, it is probable that most students were overtaught as measured in contact hours. With teaching costs more visible, a shift from five courses per year to four courses per year can be considered in both educational and economic terms. Educational considerations should, on principle, take precedence. This conclusion is strengthened by the fact that the savings through reduced course load per student are likely, on analysis, to be minimal, since few courses can be eliminated and the teaching hours saved may be those of junior, lower-salaried teachers in multiple-teacher courses.

The introduction of independent work in the upper-class undergraduate years has proved a very effective step in liberal education. It is also an expensive step, if teaching costs are clearly recognized. Only by the specific assignment of an appropriate number of students to each faculty adviser and the allocation of teaching-hour credit to the adviser, perhaps four or five students per hour, can an independent-study program be more than a paper plan. The analysis of costs may cause hesitancy in introducing or extending such a program. This does not alter the conclusion that it is an educational innovation of great merit. Again, innovations, no matter how attractive, should be weighed in both educational and economic terms when critical resources are involved.

The assignment of teaching-hour credit for the supervision of doctoral dissertations involves some complications. The time required for such supervision varies among disciplines, and students vary in the amount of attention they need. It is usually the case that some professors carry heavy loads of thesis supervision and should receive proportionate teaching-hour credit for such work. Other professors, and especially younger faculty members, may have but an occasional doctoral thesis to supervise and do not need to be given credit until the demand upon their time approximates that required to supervise three or four undergraduate theses.

Any continuing analysis of manning costs will, in most institutions, indicate a persistent trend toward increased administrative duties on the part of faculty members. The administration of departments and programs has become increasingly burdensome with the growth of laboratories, interdepartmental programs of instruction, placement activities, outside consulting, organized research, and committee work in planning and coordination. The availability of current teaching-hour reports, showing all the expensive time assigned to such activity on the part of chairmen or other department members, should encourage the appointment of nonfaculty administrative assistants in those departments most needing them. It is increasingly wasteful to assign high-salaried professors to do work which a managerial housekeeper can do better. The time is past when the most critical resource of the university can be diverted from its most productive use, even though such diversion may, for some, be more welcome than they usually admit.

A discussion of the control of teaching costs cannot avoid two controversial questions which relate to the economics of higher education. Both are raised most often by persons who are more concerned about the rising costs of education in general than they are experienced in the process and administration of *liberal* education. The first is whether there has been too much insistence that effective education at the college level requires such expensive elements as small classes and individual consultation in independent work. The second is whether teaching machines of some sort, or some means of large-scale communication, cannot be used to multiply or extend the services of the teacher to larger numbers of students.

The basic issue in both questions is the degree of personal interaction between the teacher and the student which is required to truly educate—to draw forth and thereby enhance—the potentialities of the student in terms of intellectual analysis, sensitivity to values, and maturity of judgment and, in general, to assure a personal tone of attack upon the problems he will face in life. The conviction of many with long and intensive experience in a liberal approach to higher education is clear. If liberal education were the transfer of predetermined knowledge and values—a form of indoctrination in specialized or general terms—devices for the enlargement of the numbers of recipients of transferred content per teacher would be justified. If, however, liberal education is to use our accumulating knowledge and our vast heritage of the best expressions of civilized man as a *means* of enhancing the creative powers of the individual student in his contribution and self-fulfillment, then labor-saving devices, as such, have but limited application in the essential core of the process. This does not mean that liberal education cannot use television, visual aids, and computers or electronic devices yet to come as supporting *tools* in instruction just as the book, the blackboard, the test tube, and the microscope have long served. But in liberal interactive education the tool is a *subordinate* and not a substitute mechanism. It is more likely to add to cost than to reduce it. It may be a very necessary adjunct, but it is not to any significant degree either labor-saving or cost-saving in the way it might be in the teaching of a conforming skill.

The conclusion that effective *liberal* education can obtain but very limited economies through the use of labor-saving devices is based on a continuing review of the widespread developments in educational technology. For an economist whose subject of study has long been industrial organization, it is not easy to conclude that the most expensive kind of higher education cannot reduce its costs to some reasonable degree by what has made American industry so successful. But those who carry over the aura of the marvelous economies in manpower which industry has attained to their consideration of higher education fail to give weight to a great difference in purpose. Industry deals with a useful product which can be multiplied indefinitely once a practical design and a method of production can be implemented. Education, as it proceeds beyond the transmission of basic knowledge and skills, deals with individuals who are increasingly unique in their response and potentialities. Education is a highly complex interaction, not a process of production. The only instrument so far discovered which can assure interaction at the levels of sensitivity, intuition, judgment, and enthusiasm which high intellectual potential warrants is a human being of specialized capacity and professional dedication. A book may be read, but discussion enriches understanding. A lecture may inform, but it needs to be supplemented in some degree by the opportunity for more intensive, two-way interchange of ideas.

Liberal education is the education of the human personality in its largest and most complex sense. It requires the mysterious, direct impact of personality upon personality in some reasonable proportion to be truly effective. One cannot argue a subtle moral question with a television screen. Even the great scientist, in the words of Whitehead, does not discover in order to know, but rather knows in order to discover. Liberal education at all levels is individual growth, not content; it is process, not product, except in terms of a total personality. The responses of the mind and spirit are far too subtle to be conformed to the technology of the moment, no matter how impressed we become with the marvels of an electronic age.

$\backsim$ *4* $\backsim$

ORGANIZED
RESEARCH,
COMPUTER
USE,
AND
OVERHEAD

With the outbreak of World War II, university research in science and engineering moved out of the calm waters of academic harbors into the rough seas of national security and international competition. The impact of the war, with the development of the atomic bomb and many other science-based devices and strategies, was repeated in lesser degree by the wave of concern which accompanied the revelation of the progress Russia had made in producing a Sputnik. University research in science and engineering became a big and critical operation, never to return to the simple and informal way of life of the past. More recently, social science research has been caught up in national involvement. For the university and its officers, the recognition that university research is a critical national resource has created both grave responsibilities and sticky problems.

Among the many problems created by the great expansion of organized research in the postwar period, three warrant special attention. They will serve to illustrate the complex interaction of financial and educational factors which develops as a university is caught up in the accelerating momentum of scientific and technological change. They are: (a) the control and administration of sponsored research; (b) the control and financing of computer services; and (c) the general problem of measuring and recovering overhead costs in a university.

a. The Control of Sponsored Research

The central problem for the university in the control of organized, sponsored research in which teams of teacher-scholars, senior and junior research personnel, and other supporting staff work together in a common mission is again the persistent problem of balancing the countervailing forces of differentiation and integration. Individual professors can move off in diverse directions in research without tipping the boat. As long as their individual efforts complement, in general, their field of teaching and do not involve external commitments of long duration, there is likely to be a moving equilibrium of research interests which reflects the evolving curriculum of the university, department by department. But a government contract of considerable dimensions may create a new research salient into some specialized area of interest to the sponsors but not related to the predetermined educational mission of the university. The size of the salient gives it its critical effect. Therefore, the area covered, the character of the mission, its relevancy to the growth of the discipline and of those who profess it, as well as the degree of mutual reinforcement between the research effort and fundamental instruction, must all be carefully evaluated. The contract may induce a constructive change in the university's general mission. It may, on the other hand, start the university down the primrose path of becoming a job shop for applied research for a miscellaneous clientele of paying customers. To maintain balance and integrity in its mission and organization in the face of most tempting opportunities to differentiate in many questionable directions, the university must take the initiative in establishing policy, administrative structure, and procedures for the control of organized, sponsored research. Since the growth of such research may affect the total posture of the university, it is well to assure that the policy established has received the full consideration of the faculty, the administration, and the trustees, and that it be stated in fundamental yet lucid terms. To illustrate the kind of statement needed, the following extract from the "Rules and Procedures of the Faculty of Princeton University" may be helpful:

> Princeton University has based its adoption of these policies for sponsored research upon the fact that it is dedicated to the following primary and essential objectives:
>
> 1. The education of undergraduate, graduate, and post-doctoral students.
> 2. The advancement of knowledge through research and scholarship.
> 3. The preservation and dissemination of knowledge.
> 4. The advancement and protection of the public interest and public welfare.
>
> It will be the policy of the University, the University Research Board, the departments, and members of the Faculty involved to consider the merits of any proposal for sponsored research based upon the following criteria:
>
> 1. The research should fit within the framework of the four primary and essential objectives of the University cited earlier.
> 2. The research should be soundly based and give promise of a significant contribution to knowledge, and the personnel involved should be qualified and enthusiastic.
> 3. The research should be proposed and carried out within a regular department of the University, or through the

cooperation of several departments, and be led by a member of the Faculty.

4. The research should not extend the activities of the department or departments involved too much, increasing the quantity of research at the cost of quality or to the detriment of undergraduate or graduate education.

5. Adequate facilities should be available or provisions should be made for funds to make them available.

6. There should be a good prospect of employing any additional professional or non-professional personnel required within the limits of existing salary scales and personnel policy.

7. The budget should be adequate for the work proposed, including allowance for contingencies and possible salary increases.

8. Provision should be made for any University funds required, either in the form of direct costs or indirect expenses computed in accordance with usual University practice.

9. If the research is to involve Governmental security regulations and classification, it should conform with the 'Report and Faculty Resolutions with Regard to Security and Classification in Government Sponsored Research' approved by the Faculty on May 4, 1953.

10. The terms of any contract, grant, or gift to cover the research should, insofar as possible, permit flexible operation under regular University policies and procedures, permit free publication of results (except where the requirements of national security dictate otherwise), reimburse the indirect expenses as well as the direct costs of the research, conform to the principles of the University Patent Policy and in general permit the University to exercise administrative control and responsibility for the work.

Many of the caveats in this detailed statement of policy may appear to be little more than those which any good academic administrator would take for granted. It must be remembered, however, that creative scientists are not always accustomed to weighing the organizational considerations involved in their proposals. It is well, therefore, to provide a checklist which both those who initiate proposals and those who review them can have clearly in mind. As with all such statements of policy, the proof of wisdom lies in day-to-day administration.

In order to implement such a policy, a highly responsible and continuously active review board should be established, advisory to the president, and served by a full-time administrative director and staff. All substantial proposals for sponsored research developed by individual professors and recommended by their departments should be carefully reviewed by the board. Full opportunity for discussion between proposers of projects and the board, or a sub-panel thereof, should be afforded. From time to time, the board or its staff should review the total program of sponsored research in each department or area. Administrative procedures to expedite proposals of minimal size, and yet to assure full board review of projects of larger size or involving questions of policy, can be developed.

In the establishment of a university research board, it is essential that all the major areas of the university be represented, not only those areas, such as science or engineering, in which major projects occur. The board represents the full faculty of the institution and its concern with the total mission of the institution. In addition to professors elected by the general faculty from each major area, appropriate senior administrative officers should sit *ex officio*. The chairman of the board should be a full-time university officer at the level of a senior dean, appointed by the president and responsible to him. The secretary of the board should be a director of research administration who, with his staff, implements the policies of the board.

Since sponsored research, especially that supported by governmental agencies, involves detailed procedures in respect to proposal statements, budgeting, reporting, and extensions which may become burdensome and frustrating to the professor in charge, the administrative arm of the university research board should provide procedural assistance whenever needed. The administrative staff should retain, however, a service approach and avoid assuming the initiative in developing new proposals. By rendering a supporting service, they help to offset the natural concerns of some enthusiastic project leaders when they find it necessary to come within both university policies and rules and those of sponsoring agencies.

The staff of a university research office comes to have increasing knowledge of the effectiveness of project leaders and their supporting groups in managing a project, in keeping it within the budget, and in making proper reports. Not all teacher-scholars who develop a challenging idea have the capacity to lead a research team in testing the idea. While the staff attached to the university research board should not administer any particular research project, it should be ready to recommend the appointment of administrative assistants, employed within the department or project, to provide managerial support to a project leader.

A university research board and its administrative staff come to have a strategic function in advising the president and his senior administrators on the advisability of approving not only proposals for research where a government agency or corporation may provide support, but also those where grants from foundations are needed. It is probably advisable to avoid channeling through the board the applications of professors for grants for leave pay or research support for their individual, "solo" endeavors, but a proposal to a foundation for any considerable sum should be reviewed by a central office of the university to avoid departure from stated policy or the unwise proliferation of applications to a particular foundation or other potential donor. The research board, because of its knowledge of the total research effort of the faculty, is an appropriate advisory agency. Its recommendations should evaluate individual proposals in relation to the total mission of the university and to the university's best use of its critical resources of faculty manpower, administrative talent, space, and supporting services.

The thorough integration of sponsored or other externally supported research within the university will not prove a happy state for some proponents of large-scale endeavors. Some universities have been forced by the requirements of national security to organize semi-autonomous operations to carry on large and complex projects. Others have drifted into a multiplication of institutes and programs whose connection with the university ranges from direct to distant. For some types of institutions, already serving multiple purposes in their state or community, this may be a necessary, and even a satisfactory, way of life. But for the liberal university as here defined, such a diffusion of aims and responsibilities brings serious hazards. These concern not only confusion in terms of mission, but a host of problems in organizational structure and relations, appointments, comparative salaries, faculty status, duty time, tenure, benefits, and privileges. A university is already a form of human organization which needs all the integrating influences which strong leadership and common policies can provide. To encourage atomization by setting up units whose relationships to the university organization are tenuous seems to be courting institutional disintegration, or at least a condition where the university becomes a financial holding company for a miscellaneous aggregation of intellectual and cultural endeavors.

Even with close integration, large-scale research projects produce sticky problems in personnel administration. Should qualified senior staff members in research programs be given faculty rank, voting privileges, or tenure? If such status and rights are not given them, should such personnel receive a somewhat higher salary to compensate for them? If their appointment is for the duration of a project, should they be given some assurance of further employment or of reasonable notice of termination? Should staff members teach occasionally, and if so, with what title and with what control over their courses? The status, benefits, and privileges of research staff members can become the focus of many worrisome issues. If sponsored research is to continue to be a part of university operations, a highly qualified and motivated staff is essential. Yet the university can risk neither its financial solvency nor its organizational integrity as an educational institution by affording tenure and voting privileges to those not engaged in its central and predominating mission.

The only workable approach to the problems of personnel administration arising with the large research staffs now necessary appears to be to establish a separate, carefully designed hierarchy of research ranks with a full set of policies, rules, and procedures paralleling those for members of the faculty. Appropriate ranks might be, for example, "senior research physicist," "research physicist," "research associate," and "research assistant," roughly paralleling the normal academic ranks from professor to instructor. If the title "research associate" is assigned to postdoctoral students on limited appointment, the title "staff member" might be used for junior personnel continuing for longer periods. The policies, rules, and procedures related to each research rank will vary from institution to institution. The important contribution which such framing conditions should afford is that the members of a university research staff understand fully that they are valued partners in a significant enterprise and that their status, rights, and compensation are the subject of both general and individual consideration by the central administration.

To make a parallel personnel administration for the research staff effective requires the establishment, also, of a separate, central personnel office. The officer in charge must deal with many problems specifically related to professionally trained specialists and not found in general staff administration. Because his work is closely parallel to that of the dean of faculty, or a similar educational officer, the administrator should be under the dean's immediate supervision. This association adds to the function an element of academic status which is not overlooked by those whom the administrator serves. An effective personnel officer for research staff can, through constant study of conditions inside and outside the university and by sympathetic yet equitable treatment of all individuals, make a wise structure of policies and rules a source of morale, motivation, and security for a valuable but sensitive group of people whom the university greatly needs in fulfilling its expanded mission.

b. The Control of Computer Use

In the past decade, another development in science and engineering has added complications to the academic administrator's life. This is the rapid proliferation of the computer. While the shadow of the coming computer age has fallen across many areas of instruction and administration, as well as of research, the most intense issues of support and control fall in the area of research. No matter how extensive the battery of computers available on a campus today, the demand for time and service usually exceeds supply. It will mount at an overwhelming rate. The question facing the university becomes, What part of the university's limited resources shall be allocated to computer purchase or rentals? Further, how shall computer time be assigned if all users cannot be satisfied? Does the determining of priorities invade the rights of the teacher-scholar to exercise his academic freedom in his method of research as well as in his choice of subject? Should the professor who can obtain a grant or contract to pay for computer time be permitted to squeeze out the professor who can't pay for time? Will outside funds, rather than the cherished freedom and initiative of the faculty, subtly determine the subject and effectiveness of university scholarship and research? The effort to safeguard institutional and faculty self-determination by the control of sponsored research at the front door may now have to be extended to prevent an expensive new instrument of research from exercising undue influence through the back door.

The ideal way to handle the invasion of the computer upon the academic scene is to provide time and supporting service on computers in the same way that library service is assured. This involves the addition of heavy expenditures to be absorbed as university overhead, for both professors and students engaged in unsponsored research and those who are supported by external funds. In the latter case, the percentage overhead charge could be assigned to the budget of the contract or grant and thereby recovered. The overhead chargeable to unsponsored research (or instruction) would need to be absorbed in the same way that library or other services are assumed.

The obstacle to such an ideal policy is the objection of federal agencies to the assignment of computer costs to overhead rather than to each specific contract or grant. Government accountants appear to perfer precise budgeting of computer costs even though this may lead to great difficulties in research planning and higher eventual costs through under-use of expensive equipment as particular budgets fail to conform to a predetermined, overall average use. The more fundamental objection of agency representatives appears to be that reimbursement as overhead is in some questionable way helping the university in general rather than paying for service rendered. That the government is already involving the university in many unreimbursed standby costs, such as those involved in the assurance of tenure and in the long-time development of faculty, does not seem to concern governmental officers who want discrete and precisely compensated services year by year without concern for their future availability.

Even though universities are forced to assign specific charges for computing to government-sponsored research, contract by contract, the counsel of wisdom appears to be to maintain the principle of overhead-charging for computer services to the fullest extent possible, and especially for internally supported research. Because of great expense, there may be a need for faculty supervision to prevent some few overenthusiastic members from abusing freedom by absorbing unreasonable amounts of time and service. Some control will probably be needed, but it should be exercised by colleague authority within the faculty, through an appropriate committee of fellow teacher-scholars. To have computer use in specific instances determined by accountants or even by general administrators seems a reversal of the general policy of a liberal university: to enhance academic freedom to the greatest degree that *general* resources permit.

c. The General Problem of Overhead Costs

The lack of understanding between the university and the representatives of government in respect to the computation of charges for computer use arises from the general problem of assessing reasonable overhead costs for government-sponsored research or for any particular, current activity within a university. As a perpetual and dynamic institution, a university is constantly developing talent for the years ahead. In a highly specialized and rapidly developing field of science, such as astrophysics, for example, it is very apparent that the responsible user of a professor's hard-won knowledge this year has a stake in the developing capacity of his advanced students to add to that knowledge in future years. The true cost of a *continuing* flow of creative contribution is not therefore limited to the time that a professor spends working on a project, but includes the time and effort he spends in assuring the talent needed to sustain the momentum of creative discovery in his field. In graduate education in experimental science and engineering today, it is increasingly difficult and arbitrary to draw a precise line between instruction and research.

The close interrelation between current contribution and the future potential contribution is fundamental to the nature of the university. It is not limited to science alone but is basic to a proper analysis of cost versus service rendered in any of the university's continuing activities which require highly specialized talent. The same condition exists in all well-managed enterprises but without the unique degree of responsibility to society which a university must assume. The industrial corporation contracting with government would be foolish to overlook its costs of assuring a developing capacity in its executive and technical staff to fulfill future and more demanding contracts. A university is obligated to develop not only future talent for itself in serving the government, but also the scarcest kind of talent needed by industry as industry moves ahead to new fields.

The government's efforts to separate out costs related to an arbitrary present from those related to the future and its refusal to recognize the latter costs can be questioned in terms of both sound economics and its effect on the vitality of the country's universities. There is, of course, some limit to what the government should pay for the continuing availability of the service it needs. But this is a matter of judgment and public policy and not of detailed bookkeeping. This the government recognizes in financing its own research in a wide range of fields. It would be the part of statesmanship to deal with universities on an equally farsighted basis.

The considerations of time span and flow of contribution in the determination of the "overhead" costs of university services reach back into the past as well as forward into the future. The university has invested heavily over many years in building the faculty and the organized arrangements which make possible a service currently rendered. Further, it has involved itself in assurances of tenure to maintain effective teams of specialists over long periods of time. The standby costs of an electric power system are recognized to be as real as any other costs. Standby costs are also very real in the economics of a university in assuring adequate faculty manning and the availability of other resources such as libraries and laboratories. The outside user may want the services of a particular professor or to borrow a particular book without recognition of the costs of building and maintaining a large reservoir of talent or books from which he may meet his very special and immediate need.

There is still another characteristic of the university which makes difficult the precise assessment of the true cost of any particular service and which suggests that more than conventional accounting is involved. Any organized endeavor depends upon a combination of line and staff personnel and services to assure effectiveness. The overhead costs for these services are readily recognized. But in a university, as a normal way of life, there is a mutual reinforcement of specialists in any field by a widening circle of colleague interaction which can never be neatly measured in time, energy, or cost. An experimental physicist may gain helpful advice from other experimental physicists or from theoretical physicists, mathematicians, astrophysicists, chemists, or engineers. The particular scientist rendering service may be the lens bringing knowledge or intuition to focus on a particular project, but the sources of that knowledge and intuition may be manifold, not only currently, but over years past. No one would assume that such contributions can be or should be precisely measured. Rather, as a part of the warp and woof of university activity, they indicate the special degree of difficulty one finds in trying to make the conventional pattern of accounting fit the cloth of creative research in a university.

Finally, a well-managed university in a time of rising costs is constantly trying to economize in the use of supporting staff. A means of assuring economy is to balance available manpower as closely as possible in each department with a complex of services required for instruction, research, administration, and maintenance. To require a secretary or a laboratory curator to keep a detailed work record of services performed so that the proper account can be charged is not likely to add to economy or efficiency. More important, the separation of services performed for the general mission of the university and those in the interest of an outside contractor, whether in bits and pieces or on full-time assignment, is not conducive to a common sense of mission and of mutual reinforcement in an institution peculiarly dependent upon motivation and response rather than on job specifications, work records, and time clocks. The pressures toward differentiation are already a problem for the university to contain. It is unfortunate that the accounting requirements of the government, when it sponsors university research, should add to these pressures.

5

FACULTY
SALARIES
AND
BENEFITS

a. Special Conditions Affecting University Policy

In determining its policies and procedures in compensating its faculty, a university faces many conditions which differ significantly from those normally found in industrial or business enterprises. It may be helpful to identify these special conditions before discussing the best ways to adjust to them.

1. Because of the nature of the educational process, there is no way to measure the value of an individual pro-

fessor's services by what he "produces" in terms of an indentifiable, measurable "product." The value of the total service of a university bears little relation to its tuition charges, and the value of the service of an individual professor is even further removed. Therefore, faculty compensation systems are uniquely oriented to the relative qualities of the individual, not his "product," and are limited in liberality by a total "wages fund" drawn from sources which the individual can do little to enhance.

2. A university faculty is a complex and fluid organization of highly qualified members of a learned profession covering a wide spectrum of specific disciplines and discrete areas within disciplines which are normally subject to change. Positions of unique specialization are common, not exceptional. The market for persons well qualified to fill such positions is often extremely narrow in both supply and demand, even on a national basis. Further, the contribution and potential of individuals of high talent in many specialized areas can be competently evaluated only with the advice of a small number of mature colleagues in the same specialty within the university or throughout the country.

3. The organization of the university is in the nature of a system of "partnerships," usually in the structural form of departments; therefore, personnel procedures must be designed to assure adequate participation, under the leadership of a chairman, of all those who have common responsibility for the long-run effectiveness of the particular partnership and, except for outside appointments, who are senior in rank to the person evaluated.

4. To maintain common standards of evaluation and to implement an integrated and equitable personnel system, however, the recommendations of departments must be reviewed at a school and universitywide level by representatives of both the faculty and the administration. A professor is both a member of a department and a mem-

ber of a university faculty which has corporate responsibilities. There is need, therefore, for administrative procedures which balance the initiative and judgment of the specialists within a department and the department as a structural subunit primarily concerned in its direct interests, with the judgment of those who are concerned with school and universitywide standards, effectiveness, and equity.

5. In the operation of a university, for reasons outlined earlier, a president must provide both leadership and judgment in respect to the appointment and advancement of faculty members. Since he is the person finally responsible to the trustees for the character, integrity, and effectiveness of the university in fulfilling its determined mission, he must have the final decision on all significant personnel actions to a much larger degree than a comparable executive in industry or business. Therefore, all procedures prior to a president's decision are essentially in the form of advice to him in making his recommendations to the board as the legally competent, appointing authority.

6. While titles are important in most structured organizations, the hierarchical ranks from instructor to full professor and the various associated ranks are of exceptional significance in an academic community. Standardized across the university and related to personal qualification and attainment rather than to precise function or authority, they indicate merit, status, and tenure with marked visibility. Their existence and wise assignment provide a means of encouraging wholesome motivation and the assumption of increasing responsibility in a profession where attainment is otherwise difficult to demonstrate. (Few persons outside the academic community are able to judge the standing of a medieval historian or a plasma physicist, but they readily recognize that a professor outranks an associate professor.)

7. Since the effectiveness of a university is so highly depen-

dent upon the motivation of its teacher-scholars in their free and responsible fulfillment of professional obligations, and since persons who deal in ideas and values are more likely than most people to be introspective and disturbed by any appearance of injustice, the compensation system of a university must be carefully safeguarded against any suspicion of carelessness, bias, bureaucratic rigidity, or personal favoritism. The inequitable treatment of individuals or of departments, or any sense of unwarranted deprivation or preferment, can lead to a subtle but persistent loss in morale and contribution. Even small differentials in salary become important when other indications of relative merit are not readily apparent.

8. A large segment of a university faculty, and especially those at the higher salary levels and of the greatest strategic value to the institution, are on permanent tenure and will, in most cases, continue with the university for their working span of life. By long tradition, their salary rates will continue to rise throughout their employment even though their financial needs and their relative contribution may be greatest in mid-career. It is most difficult, given the nature of university organization and its great reliance upon individual morale, to alter a long-established pattern of salary progression which does not fit career needs. There is justification, therefore, for a system of supplementary benefits which is especially responsive to the needs of mid-career members and their families.

9. Few professors are accustomed to business and financial procedures and to risk taking in financial terms. Few have been able to accumulate substantial savings except in annuity reserves or in their equity in a home. Yet economic security for themselves and their families at a level compatible with their professional status is of special concern, since financial worries may seriously affect intellectual tone and contribution.

10. Finally, since the effective participation of a teacher-scholar in the mission of a university requires direct and sustained interpersonal relations with colleagues and students, measures for the enhancement of a sense of community in living as well as at work appear to be justified to a greater extent than in other types of enterprise. A dynamic concept of faculty benefits cannot, therefore, be limited to individual financial needs alone but should encompass arrangements for an integrated and mutually reinforcing community, including adequate living and recreational accommodations.

It is easier to outline the special conditions faced by a university administration in developing an effective salary and benefit program for its faculty than to succeed fully in meeting these conditions. This is especially true in a time of financial stringency when every dollar must be put where it will have most effect and when there is little room for maneuver. It is the conviction of one who entered university administration from the field of industrial relations, however, that no aspect of administrative endeavor will pay better dividends for the time and energy invested than an intelligent, sensitive, and sustained attention to the equitable and adequate compensation of those who form the cutting edge of the universtiy's mission. Morale, where it is good, is likely to be taken for granted. Where it is less so for reasons, among others, of a distrust of the university's sustained interest in the personal, financial problems of its people, the results will be hidden in excessive turnover and lost opportunities for the improvement of quality, motivation, and dedication in a common effort.

b. Salary Policies and Procedures

Reflecting the conditions outlined, the general characteristics of a good compensation system can be summarized. Salary policies and the procedures in their implementation should be firmly established, although open to continuing review through the normal channels of consultation. They should be clearly stated in an appropriate publication available to all concerned. The minimum salary rates for each academic rank should be common knowledge and strictly enforced. The range of individual salaries within each rank should extend over a reasonable proportion of the spread to the next higher minimum without considerable overlap beyond. To use a promotion in rank as a substitute for full recognition of merit in salary terms undermines the value and integrity of a rank structure. To advance a member's salary clearly out of line with his assigned rank suggests that there is need for an early review of salary scales as a whole, or that a policy of convenience has replaced a courageous application of standards for promotion.

Under existing conditions in the market for high academic talent, and with the pressures of both inflation and financial stringency, any faculty salary structure must be reviewed annually. Even though an institution uses a system of step rates related to years of service, more usually in the lower ranks, salary changes related to personal experience do not compensate for those made necessary by market conditions or a rising cost of living. Where step rates do not apply and in institutions following a policy of annual, individual review in all ranks, each department must be provided with guidelines, developed after consultation by the central administration, which embody general policy in respect to prospective scales, norms in the adjustment of salaries by rank, and patterns of distribution of merit increases deemed appropriate in terms of general market conditions. In order to place as much responsibility as possible upon each department, however, it appears to be wise policy to provide each with a specific dollar budget for its total of recommended merit increases, subject to claims upon a general reserve where promotions involve larger than usual increases or where unusually severe competition is faced.

The central review of departmental recommendations for merit increases in salary, for promotions, and for significant new appointments is the critical operation in a sound personnel system. While arrangements and procedures vary widely among institutions, several elements appear to be conducive to good results. It is necessary to have carefully designed recommendation forms which require an analysis of the attributes and contributions of each person reviewed and which are to be supplemented by all relevant, supporting material such as reviews of publications or comments by persons outside the department who are in a position to judge his work.* The ordering and analysis of departmental recommendations are a major task for the dean of the faculty. It is his obligation, through repeated conferences with chairmen, to understand more completely the views and intentions of the department than written material can record. His continuing concern is to assure full and precise presentation of the factors which make the individual an increasingly valuable member of a team, such as enhanced effectiveness in teaching, scholarship, and departmental administration in appropriate balance, and not merely a comfortable and "deserving" colleague. Annual recommendation forms not only are the basis for current action by a review committee, but they form a historical record of a member's progress over the years. Among other advantages, they help in tempering the effect of sporadic outside offers upon the judgment of overanxious colleagues.

It is an important attribute of a central committee for the review of faculty advancements in salary and rank that it should bring together the key academic officers concerned and the elected representatives of the faculty. Each group contributes a valuable point of view to the demanding exercise of evaluating individuals and assigning a limited resource of funds and positions. An ideal committee is one chaired by the president with not more than four members elected by the faculty and not more than four senior academic officers, of which one, the dean of the faculty, serves as executive secretary.

In the deliberations of the central review committee, the recommendations for individuals should be compared within a department and, for senior men, should also be compared across the division and the university. While some recognition must be given to the differing national market conditions for talent in the various disciplines, the amount of departure from norms, rank by rank, for equal merit in widely different disciplines should be as

---

* Recommendation forms used at Princeton University are reproduced in the Appendix, pages 241–247.

small as possible in order to enhance a general sense of equity. While it is generally assumed that individual salaries are confidential information on a university campus, the procedures in their determination involve many people. It is the counsel of wisdom to decide each case as if the result were subject to review by all interested persons. A reputation for integrity and equity in a university's salary structure, built up by the series of decisions which are known to particular members at various times, has very real effect in building and holding a strong faculty. In contrast, a policy of granting sporadic, ad hoc differentials to highly visible individuals has hidden costs which may well offset apparent immediate gains. A growing assumption among a faculty that "prima donnas" get fancy salaries while others do the work can do much to undermine the morale of a sensitive group of people. The "star system" of the entertainment world has serious defects when transferred to academia. This does not mean that clearly earned differentials are not recognized as deserved and necessary, especially if awarded under respected procedures. It is also generally recognized that reasonable accommodation is necessary in some new appointments or in fending off an especially attractive offer. The difference between an integrated salary system and a policy of opportunism becomes evident to a faculty over time.

In the present condition of active competition for high talent in many disciplines, the external influences on salary patterns are greater than they were a decade ago. Even if an institution has been able to raise its general salary scales in parallel with its chief competitors and has maintained a program of thoroughgoing annual reviews, it cannot hope to avoid a considerable number of individual salary determinations each year which reflect alternative outside opportunities. In part, this is so because close colleagues may not recognize the growth of younger men as quickly as do professors elsewhere. Also, critical vacancies develop in other universities which are ready to pay more generously than is their usual custom in order to fill them. The most difficult kind of competition to meet is that where an institution has no orderly salary policy. The practical test of a sound salary policy is that, case by case, there will be definite limits upon the degree to which outside alternative salaries will be permitted to influence reasonably determined differentials.

In recent years, the general levels of faculty salaries, institution by institution, have become public knowledge through the published annual ratings of the American Association of University Professors. There is little question but that these ratings, by their high visibility in concerned circles, have encouraged progress in raising faculty salary levels following a long period of lagging adjustment to higher costs of living and higher earnings in industry.

As a price for a specialized kind of service in an operation little affected by technological means of increasing hourly or annual production, faculty salaries in private universities can match the progress of general salary averages in the outside world only if tuition rates are raised, endowment income is increased, or more funds are received from donors for current support. With increasingly severe competition for university-level faculty talent because of increasing student enrollments, expanded subject coverage, and extensive sponsored research, a private liberal university must exercise its corporate intelligence to enhance the attractiveness of service on its faculty. There is urgent need, therefore, to be sure that its procedures in the assignment of the funds available for faculty salaries are fully effective in sustaining quality, contribution, and morale.

c. Policy Concerning Supplementary Benefits

It has become increasingly clear that the provision of a comprehensive and adequate system of supplementary benefits by universities and colleges is not paternalism but an essential part of an assumed contract of employment. Responsible representatives of the faculty should be consulted in developing the total program, even though no formal agreement is customary or necessary. Some benefit arrangements should be compulsory where complete coverage is necessary, such as with contributory retirement protection. In other cases, noncontributory protection may be provided, assuming the right of the individual, in principle, to determine the claims he will make. Still other programs may be voluntary in respect to participation and contribution. The details of faculty benefits, both financial and nonfinancial, are many and complex, and they have been covered effectively in specialized publications, especially those sponsored by the Teachers Insurance and Annuity Association and the American Association of Colleges. It may be more helpful here, therefore, to discuss certain issues of policy which are likely to develop in the planning of a faculty benefit program rather than detailed provisions.

d. Retirement Annuity Programs

The first claim upon the funds available for faculty benefits should be for an adequate retirement annuity program. The Teachers Insurance and Annuity Association has been a bulwark of strength in helping universities, colleges and other educational institutions to meet their obligations to their teachers and to themselves in this area of personnel administration. It is believed that continuing inflation now requires many institutions to raise their sights in respect to the level of retirement annuity which will become necessary to meet the needs of the retiree or his surviving widow many years ahead. Unless such needs are met in reasonable degree, with national social security benefits included, it will become difficult to retire older professors on an orderly basis. It is a fair working hypothesis that approximately as many older members will need protection for themselves or their survivor *before* any normal retirement date as after. Therefore, the amount of protection afforded needs to be weighed in terms of the actuarial reduction in benefits which occurs when retirement or death occurs at an earlier-than-normal age.

It is believed that retirement annuity programs should be contributory, not only to raise the level of protection, but to encourage a sense of financial participation in building a life estate. In the light of increasing social security deductions, the ratio of institutional to personal contribution can well be three to one, however, especially if a graduated scale of contributions according to age is introduced. A workable scheme is to require contributions by the participants of three, four, and five percent for age groups under forty, in their forties, and fifty and over, respectively, while the institutional contributions scale rises in parallel from nine, to twelve, to fifteen percent of salary. Such graduations are intended to help match the changing pattern of need for immediately available income compared to the rising level of salary received, as members' families mature. It also puts the largest proportion of institutional funds into those individual accounts where the member is likely to be a continuing and strategic contributor to the university. However, sound policy requires that the rates for younger men should be adequate to start building reasonably sufficient reserves for them, supplementing their social security protection, no matter where they may be employed in later life. Such a plan is expensive, but it is believed to be a wise long-run investment.

The retirement annuity program which has been outlined is assumed to be entirely supplementary in its operation to the federal system of social security contributions and benefits. In judging the relative liberality of the total protection afforded the faculty member or his family throughout life, social security benefits, as well as social security taxes paid by the member and the university, are matters of serious concern. While each institution must determine the degree of liberality it can afford, it is believed that the special conditions faced by a university in designing a program for its faculty in a time of sharply rising salaries warrants a program fully supplementary to that provided under the Social Security Act, at least for the present. The adjustment which can be made in the case of permanent disability benefits will be discussed later.

A retirement annuity program is intended to provide a means for conserving the dynamic quality of a faculty as a whole as individual members advance in age. To be an effective instrument of personnel policy, both adequacy of benefits and equity in administration are essential. To avoid both uncertainty and any suspicion of inequitable treatment, the age of retirement should be fixed and firm. The precise age established is less important than its certainty and general acceptance. With the mounting costs of adequate protection for both the annuitant and a surviving spouse, as well as the growing scarcity of highly qualified manpower relative to demand, a reasonable case can be made for the use of sixty-eight as the retirement age for faculty members so far as teaching service is involved. Many institutions have, however, followed the practice of industry and business in adopting a sixty-five-year limit. Again, a distinction can be made between the conditions in a university and those in industry.

In industry, higher-salaried personnel are likely to be in administrative positions and those on lower salaries or wages in employment for which sustained mental or physical effort is required, as well as adjustment to rapidly changing methods. An older professor in a university, as distinguished from an administrative officer, is performing a service in which long-developed knowledge, wisdom, and professional intuition in dealing with students and subject matter are usually more important than the capacity for quick decision, long and sustained effort, or adjustment to rapidly changing conditions. University professors usually commence full-time productive employment later than most people and after a heavy investment in specialized preparation. The earlier displacement of older employees by industry at age sixty-five may be fully justified in the face of rapid technological change. There is serious question, however, whether higher education, with the scarcity of the specialized kind of talent it so greatly needs, should accept without serious study the conventions of industry and ignore the special characteristics of a learned profession. If it is argued that some professors become obsolete before sixty-eight, it may be suggested that this is better remedied by developmental programs throughout the professor's active career than by a general curtailment of the services of all professors before reaching an age determined by broader considerations.

While a retirement age for faculty should be firmly established and fully implemented, recall for part-time duty in rare cases of special need and unique qualification can usually be justified in terms of equity and morale. It is important that recalls be infrequent, understandable to others, and involve only "visiting," part-time status. Also, it is a sound policy that the compensation of a recalled professor be adjusted to actual duty performed without reference to his previous salary or his annuity income.

e. Insurance Programs

The standard forms of group insurance now in effect in many universities have contributed greatly to improved morale and to lessening the financial strain created by serious illness or death in the closely balanced budgets of most academic families. Anyone who has been consulted on many sad occasions over the years comes to realize that although financial help does not lessen grief when disaster comes, it prevents disaster from broadening into deep and lasting anxiety. With speedy availability of benefits and of complete advisory services, the concern of an institution is symbolized in an effective way.

In order to make sure that group life insurance benefits are automatically available in case of death, it is preferable to provide complete coverage on a noncontributory basis, at least for an amount assumed to be generally adequate. By making basic coverage noncontributory, the problem of differential costs according to age is avoided. Supplementary protection on a contributory basis can be added related to level of salary. An ideal plan would be, however, noncontributory coverage for all for an amount, beyond a common minimum, of one and one-half to two times base salary.

Insurance against medical and hospital expenses and the contingency of long-continuing disability requires an interlocking set of arrangements. A balanced program might well include:

a. A voluntary, *contributory*, group insurance program similar to that of the Blue Cross–Blue Shield type, with premiums deducted from salary in part or in full.

b. An interlocking, *noncontributory* program of major medical expense insurance such as that provided by the Teachers Insurance and Annuity Association, adjusted in the amount before benefits are payable to the type of coverage voluntarily carried under Blue Cross–Blue Shield.

c. A *noncontributory* program of permanent and total disability insurance, such as is provided by the Teachers Insurance and Annuity Association, which includes an offset to the disability benefits payable under the federal social security program.

The rationale of such a combined program is that by means of it faculty members are both more able and more ready to meet, in considerable measure, the costs of insuring against less costly illnesses. The infrequent incidence of major illness or long-continued disability, especially for younger members, reduces the likelihood of full, voluntary participation in such insurance. It is also true that a flat rate of contribution regardless of age tends to be inequitable. Since the institution cannot avoid involvement when a faculty member faces serious financial difficulties because of illness or disability, it appears to be the counsel of wisdom to provide complete, noncontributory insurance protection against major medical expenses and permanent disability. With standard benefits available to all, the university can then establish definite limits upon the continuation of regular salary payments before permanent disability insurance payments begin.

By the sympathetic, confidential, and intelligent handling of the numerous contingencies which develop in a faculty community, the personality of a university as a humane institution in which every individual counts is confirmed in the minds of far more than those immediately involved. Insurance provides the necessary mechanism by which the traditions of an institution and the understanding concern of its officers become tangibly clear to the distressed person or survivor who needs more than sympathy alone.

No matter how carefully a system of insurance is contrived, there will be uncovered areas of serious need. Even the amount of coinsurance required in health insurance programs may become an impossible burden. The availability of a president's discretionary fund helps greatly in those relatively rare situations where an uncovered dependent, a long-protracted illness, or heavy home-care expenses are involved. If chairmen and deans know that such a fund is available to back any reasonable assurance of help, they do not have to check the fine points in insurance policies before giving assurances when they do most good.

f. Faculty Housing Programs

A less usual but growing form of supplementary faculty benefit is housing assistance. Few universities have extensive faculty housing programs. Such programs involve heavy investment and sustained planning over many years. Yet the pressure of urban blight and the rise in land values and rentals in suburban areas adjacent to universities are making converts of academic administrators and trustees who formerly suggested that "company housing" was a device of industrial paternalism. The arguments for a carefully planned system of faculty housing are gaining strength each year as adjacent areas become crowded and housing costs become an important element in matching salaries to needs. Some may be summarized:

As a perpetual institution with a heavy investment in structures and attractive living space within its campus, an urban university must protect its adjacent neighborhood against decay. It can seldom move away. Faculty housing under the control of the university is an ideal means of stabilizing a considerable buffer area.

On the other hand, if a university is fortunate enough to be in an attractive suburban community, its very presence will raise housing costs sharply and put rentals or home ownership near the university out of the range of many faculty members. By land purchase and development for faculty housing, the university can hedge against the further speculative rise in land costs, and yet by replacing the homes, when needed, it can have space available for instructional facilities for many years ahead. Meanwhile the land is serving a valuable immediate use.

A university program of faculty housing can be planned to balance the proportions of smaller and larger apartment units, of larger rental houses, and of houses built by individuals under mortgage or repurchase contracts. Thus the varying needs of members through their careers as family composition changes can be met far more effectively than through reliance upon an outside, speculative real estate market. Further, change-over times, as members come and go or move within the system, can be coordinated. Newly hired members do not have to be left to search out housing in distant suburbs or to delay moving until chance vacancies occur. The advantages of a well-planned internal market for faculty housing become more evident as the program begins to meet a reasonable proportion of a faculty's need for adequate accommodation.

The concept of community, especially in a liberal, residential university, has been stressed repeatedly. Faculty housing reinforces this concept in an aspect of university life where it has been taken too much for granted, despite the influences of growing size and differentiation of discipline. With the present wide spread of disciplines, professors have many different interests and avocations. Living together in adjacent faculty housing areas affords rich opportunities for interesting and congenial neighborhood life. There develops a common concern in community and university affairs, education, scholarship, and ideas. There is also a diminution of the pressures "to keep up with the Joneses," whose interests are likely to be expressed in terms which academic salaries may not meet.

A university should not embark on an extensive program of faculty housing without thorough study of long-run needs, costs, and the requirements for effective administration. While the total operation must be as intelligently managed as any commercial development, the purpose of enhancing faculty strength and morale must be constantly kept in mind. A faculty housing system, to be effective, cannot be looked upon as a profitable ancillary enterprise to provide a normal return on endowment funds. Rather it is primarily an investment to enhance the effectiveness of the university's most critical resource and means of service, its faculty. The trustees of the university should fully realize the distinction. While a business operation in day-to-day procedures, it is essentially a personnel operation in mission and in the climate of the service it renders. Therefore, the policies under which a faculty housing system operates should be determined jointly by the chief educational officer and the chief financial officer under the president, with full consultation, when pertinent, with an appropriate faculty committee. It is also important that a special administrative department covering it be established, distinct from that responsible for the general buildings and facilities of the university.

g. Faculty Children's Tuition Scholarships

Just as a system of faculty housing can help the individual professor to make a rising, career-long pattern of income fit a changing family need, so another valuable supplementary benefit, faculty children's tuition scholarships, can help in the adjustment. It is the heavy expense of children in college which often puts the most severe strain on the budget of an academic family. Such families assume that a college education is a necessity and that its absence is a serious deprivation. Therefore, as a part of a total scheme of faculty benefits, programs for faculty children's tuition scholarships have been developed.

Lifted out of the context of the special conditions which exist in university personnel administration, such tuition grants might suggest a climate of paternalism. There would be more justification for this criticism if these grants were not made a part of an established benefit program after consultation with representatives of the faculty. From the point of view of the university, such grants help meet a special problem in its competition for staff. A valuable professor in his forties with children to put through college in a time of mounting costs is peculiarly susceptible to an offer which involves a sharply increased salary for work which capitalizes on his present capacity rather than his potential contribution in the years ahead. A countering argument that one can borrow against a gradually rising salary in academia is not as persuasive as immediate assistance in meeting college costs as they develop, child by child and year by year.

A faculty children's tuition program can be adjusted to the total annual institutional appropriation possible and to the varying needs of those covered. A moderately liberal plan is one which grants $1,000 to $1,200 for each child for each year in college, limited, however, to stated tuition and general fees. The goal is to meet at least one-half of the tuition charge in a private college. It is reasonable to limit grants to children enrolled in four-year programs, since those taking shorter and more vocational courses can be assumed to create a less protracted financial strain on their families. Tuition grants are transmitted directly to the college in which the child is enrolled.

A means of meeting uncovered cases, and those where grants still leave heavy burdens, is to establish an educational loan fund providing loans of up to, perhaps, $1,000 per child per year in higher education, repayable with interest by automatic salary deductions over a period of eight or more years. This, again, spreads college costs over a period when the professor is better able to meet them.

Throughout this discussion of salaries and benefits, the emphasis has been upon policies related to faculty personnel. It is obvious that responsible academic administrators of all types should come under the same policies and programs, since no tendency for cleavage should be permitted to develop. For other staff, parallel programs for retirement annuities and insurance of various types are essential, although designed to meet their specific needs. It is probable that housing assistance will need to be limited in most institutions to faculty, senior officers, and closely related, professional research staff. Since a great majority of staff employees, unlike faculty members, were living in or near the university community *before* they became employees, it can be assumed that they have adjusted themselves to the problems of local housing. In most institutions, housing assistance to staff personnel needs to be limited to very special groups, given the heavy costs involved. Faculty children's tuition grants and loans can be extended to longer-service staff members. They are a most attractive benefit, if the added cost can be met.

Underlying the foregoing analysis of salary and benefit policy is the premise that compensation and security are fundamental and positive instruments in a sound faculty personnel policy within a framework of effective leadership and organization, and not a peripheral concern. The economic aspect of motivation is the seeking of a higher level of security through both increased income and increased protection from costly contingencies difficult to meet. In the past, there has been talk of "fringe" benefits. But the "fringe" is, and should be, an essential part of the cloth in a wise and effective compensation program in an institution which seeks to understand human needs and motives in general as well as those of its own faculty, administration, and staff.

PROBLEMS
OF
EXTERNAL
RELATIONS

PROBLEMS
OF
EXTERNAL
RELATIONS

✑ 1 ✑

RELATIONS
WITH
FEDERAL
AND
LOCAL
GOVERNMENTS

a. Relations with the Federal Government

The influence of the older liberal colleges in America upon the national government reaches back to the formation of that government. It is said that James Madison's significant insights in the drafting of the United States Constitution were much influenced by his studies with John Witherspoon at Princeton. John Adams was the first of a long line of presidents educated at Harvard. Alexander Hamilton attended Kings College, now Columbia.

The influence of the national government on the successors of these colleges, now liberal universities, has a much shorter history.

The financial assistance given through the Land Grant Act a century ago was primarily aimed at more practical requirements than the older liberal arts colleges were assumed to meet. But since World War II, with the recognition of the critical need for advanced scientific and engineering knowledge and for highly talented specialists in scores of fields, the concern of the national government with the institutions which could provide these resources has had marked effect upon their way of life. Since the older, liberal universities proved to be among the best sources of highly expert talent and critical research findings, they were caught up in a flood of governmental interest. The influence of liberal institutions upon government through their alumni and faculties has grown steadily over the years, but the influence of the government upon the institutions themselves has become far more direct and tangible.

The concern of the national government has now expanded to the whole process of higher education as the recognition of the critical place of educated talent in national security and progress has become clear. The government's interest in research findings has been implemented through specific contracts and grants, negotiated on an ad hoc basis, involving particular individuals or groups. The newer interest in a broad flow of students through all stages of higher education, however, has posed questions of policy for the older, private university which involve its traditional and central purpose, liberal education for leadership.

The development of review panels in the assignment of government contracts and grants for research has served as a protective buffer mechanism between the government agency as a purchaser of services and the university which, through its faculty, provides those services. A panel of independent specialists advising the government agency selects, not a university, but the professor within a discipline, wherever he may be, most competent in their judgment to produce valuable results. The government is spared the delicate task of selecting the university, as such, to which it assigns funds for service rendered. The university, as an institution, is protected from the direct pressure to tailor its academic policies to a governmentally determined market as distinct from internal considerations. The panel system has, in general, worked well; but, emphasizing the quality and proved performance of individuals, it has tended to concentrate contracts and grants in institutions where strong faculties were already present rather than spreading such contracts and grants throughout the full spectrum of institutions at various stages of development.

The policy of contract assignment on the basis of the evaluated competency of individual professors to perform, rather than as an aid to the development of new faculty potential, has had an important influence upon the climate of relationships between the liberal university and the federal government. Under a panel system of assignment, a university is assumed to determine its areas of interest and faculty growth for itself, with governmental interest secondary. If contract assignment became a means of "subsidizing" new ventures in faculty development in institutions of varying strength, the government would come to exercise direct influence upon university policy throughout the country and, at the same time, would become exposed to all the political pressures which presumed "subsidies" encourage. The true cost to the university in fulfilling government contracts is discussed elsewhere.

Long observation has led to the conviction that the system of assigning research contracts on the basis of the proven competency of individual professors is not only in the interest of the government, but is a necessary means of assuring a climate of free enterprise and independent initiative in the universities. Pluralistic initiative in the discovery of new knowledge and in gaining a fuller understanding of truth is a precious ingredient in our national life.

As the interest of the national government has expanded into increasing the general flow of qualified young people through higher education, the private liberal university must look to some comparable device which keeps federal appropriations from influencing its free and self-reliant determination of its way of life. In the case of contract research and grants, the protective device has proved to be the concept that the government is concerned with the services of *individual professors* who have been independently selected to fulfill the total mission of the university. In the case of government support related to instruction, the parallel device is the concept that the government is concerned with helping the *individual student* admitted to the university under its independently determined policies in respect to qualification and number. Such an approach can cover both undergraduate loans and scholarships and graduate fellowships. While government aid to students may permit many who could not otherwise afford higher education to obtain it, and indirectly may make some specialized graduate programs more feasible, it does not create the pressure for accommodation to government influence which direct institutional grants for general use would involve.

A third area of governmental involvement in the activities of the liberal university is the provision of assistance in building structures such as dormitories, graduate student housing, or research facilities. Here, again, the necessary aim is to prevent the availability of federal funds from becoming a primary rather than a secondary consideration in university decisions. It is unfortunately true that the easier it is to build buildings, the harder it is to avoid accretion in numbers to fill them, whether in terms of students, professors, or programs. The need for balance and restraint is obvious.

The three principal areas in which the liberal university is now affected by the growing interest of the federal government in higher education have been outlined in very simple terms in order to illustrate the kind of problems now faced. The complications in terms of organized research and overhead costs have already been discussed. The administration of student loans and grants under federal rules involves many detailed adjustments. Federal standards and limitations concerning construction projects raise many sticky issues. But, in general, the private, liberal university is learning to work with the many agencies of the federal government as an independent, self-directed institution in terms of mission and policy. The more obvious pressures for conforming to bureaucratic influences may have been controlled through countervailing arrangements and persistent vigilance, but more fundamental problems may lie ahead.

To suggest the nature of these problems, two questions may

be posed. What would be the effect on the private university if the funds now appropriated by the federal government for fundamental research, various specialized instructional projects, student assistance, and construction should cease to be available? Further, given sharply rising costs, will the private, liberal university be able to finance itself and still limit its participation in federally sponsored programs to those areas where "arm's-length" arrangements are possible?

The most difficult problem that the private, liberal university would face if federal appropriations in its field of interest were seriously curtailed is that of supporting the expanded faculty, particularly in science and engineering, which federally sponsored research has encouraged. While sharp reductions could be made in the number of junior faculty appointed, the presence of many senior faculty members on tenure appointment involves a continuing financial obligation which must be met. It would be both difficult and wasteful to shift older, more specialized faculty members to the teaching assignments left uncovered because of a depleted junior staff. The per-student cost of instruction would rise drastically and the upward flow of maturing talent would be seriously curtailed. The university would face serious educational and financial problems during a long period of adjustment.

A second and related problem would be the elimination of part-time positions in sponsored research which now help large numbers of graduate students in science and engineering, in particular, to finance their advanced education and the cost of their research. This problem would be all the more serious if government fellowship grants were also reduced. Few graduate students today are supported by their parents. Again, a flow of valuable talent would be interrupted until alternative financing could be developed.

Federal programs for aid to undergraduates are a more recent development. Their elimination would require a private institution to limit its admission of needy students to those whom it is able to assist from its own funds. Most liberal universities with selective admissions would be forced regretfully to shift the balance of their admissions in some degree toward those candidates who can pay their own way, even though somewhat less qualified. Their help to the underprivileged would be reduced.

Finally, the loss of federal assistance in building construction would be of lesser effect. Universities are accustomed to delays in balancing space needs. The loss would be in the ready adjustment to reasonably determined growth.

In sum, the probable effects of a possible curtailment of federal appropriations for fundamental university research and for other aspects of university activity suggest that the federal government has already limited the freedom of the liberal institution to be financially self-reliant. Even if total federal appropriations remained unchanged, a shift in the method of assignment of university contracts and grants for research to some politically determined formula of egalitarian, geographical distribution would have serious effects upon the older, stronger institutions. It must be the hope of those concerned with the future of the private, liberal university which has, after long years of self-reliant growth, become involved in arrangements with a financially powerful government, that abrupt and arbitrary changes in policy will be avoided. The university can develop many specific measures to assure its freedom of decision, program by program. It cannot, in a time of sharply rising costs, protect itself from the financial risk of a sudden termination of a policy of mutually beneficial cooperation in meeting the needs of the country.

The second question posed is still more difficult to answer. Can the private, liberal university avoid *greater* dependence upon government if endowment income, tuition fees, and gifts fail to keep up with rising salaries and costs? Some private universities have become public institutions. Various methods of subsidization have been proposed. Perhaps some new formula can be designed to insulate a flow of funds from a flow of influence upon a supposedly independent institution. If the distribution of government funds is broadened to include more than the support and instruction of the *individual* student, the services of the *individual* professor working on a research contract or grant, the financing of a *particular*, specialized program, or the construction of a *specific* building, a critical point of no return may be passed. If no other form of influence developed in the decisions of the independent, private institution, the risk of a sudden reduction in public financial support would become a very serious concern. It would become most difficult, it is believed, to avoid some degree of accommodation to the views of those most instrumental in assuring adequate and continuing financial support. This is not to deny the wisdom of congresses and legislatures, but to suggest that, somewhere along the line, the valuable attribute of freedom and pluralistic initiative in American private higher education would be impaired. It can only be hoped that those who are now the major support of the private, liberal university—its alumni and friends —will remain firmly convinced that such impairment should be avoided.

Freedom to pursue a self-determined philosophy of education even at mounting cost, must be bought at a price. The price must be paid by those who best understand the special contributions of the independent, liberal university in a time when the forces toward conformity in American life are strengthened by the concentration of great financial power in our national government. No matter how wise the elected representatives in a democratic government may be, they must, over time, reflect the general consensus of our citizens in the services which they support. To do otherwise would be a denial of principle in our political system, as well as a poor way to get reelected.

b. Relations with Local Governments

A liberal university must learn to live with its neighbors and an increasingly complex system of local government. It is a long and difficult course of study. The university administrator is sometimes inclined to paraphrase the remark of the greatest teacher the world has known by suggesting that a national university is not without honor save in its own community. High talent and fundamental knowledge are national and worldwide needs, but the university as a means of meeting them puts ever-increasing pressures on local housing, schools, streets, hospitals, and other services and utilities. It also introduces a constantly changing community within a community which does not always conform readily to local customs. Unlike a community college or even a state university, a national, liberal university can do little through instructional services for local residents to justify its presence. It is likely that much of its activity in both teaching and scholarship lies in areas which appear to be impractical or obscure. A town of a few thousand may show pride in and affection for its local college; but as the town becomes a city and the college a great university, it is hard to love a neighbor whose concerns reach far afield from the daily life of the community.

It is a significant and hopeful sign, however, that the faculties of liberal universities, particularly in the social sciences, are now finding that some of the most challenging problems for study are close at home and not in Washington. Humanists and scientists deal in ageless or abstract aspects of learning, but the social scientist is concerned with organized society wherever it exists. The problems of state and local government, urban planning, race relations, employment, welfare, housing, and education can be studied close at hand by both professors and students. Involvement in a local community as a part of interactive, liberal education and as a means of gaining new knowledge in a highly complex field may have valuable results not only in helping to solve urgent local problems, but in proving that a university recognizes the obligations of a good neighbor. It requires, however, the hard work, patience, understanding, and judgment of the professional specialist and the avoidance of the zeal and self-assurance of the impassioned amateur whether young or old.

Whether understood or not, a university can make a strong case for the belief that its economic contribution to the local community is large even though its direct educational contribution may be limited. Despite the fact that its property used for direct educational purposes is exempt from taxes, there is probably no type of enterprise which provides a more stable flow of income to its community. Funds accruing from endowment income, tuition fees, grants, and gifts from a steady flow of imported purchasing power to be distributed locally in professional and staff salaries, which, on average, compare favorably in level and regularity with those of most employed groups. Further distribution occurs in the local purchases of the university and in the payment of taxes on nonexempt property. Additional funds come to the community through the expenditures of students and visitors. It is this combination of flows of purchasing power which is the true source of the solid, taxpaying capacity of many of the business units and residents in a university community. The precise point at which a flow of funds is tapped for public use is far less important than the fact that there is a large and steady flow available for tapping.

A university enhances the economy of its community in other ways. With farsighted planning, it can do much to stabilize or increase land values in its neighborhood. Its cultural activities make its neighborhood a desirable place to buy a home and live. Research organizations are attracted by the presence of an academic community and of its library and laboratory facilities. More directly, a university may make grants for specific services, such as for police and fire protection or for health and sanitation. It may provide roads, park areas, recreational facilities, and meeting places which supplement without cost those of the community. Apart from any visibility it may give its community throughout the world, a university can be an important resource in a local economy.

But neighborhood relations are not always improved by generous contributions, especially if they are indirect, impersonal, or intangible. The long-continued presence of the university leads to the assumption that its facilities and resources are automatically available for public use until withdrawal of some customary privilege leads to inconvenience. The general and positive contributions of the university may be less a factor in community relations than year-by-year developments which affect particular people or community services. The crowding of schools, the closing of a road, the building of a high-rise structure, or the "too-active" participation of faculty and students in some local political situation may be the immediate cause of irritation. The importance of the particular as opposed to the general is a common characteristic in the short swings of public opinion that normally occur in most areas of community life. Yet a pervasive and continuing climate of mutual accommodation will do much to create a frame of reference in which differences can be resolved.

The best approach that a university can follow appears to be: to study constantly and intelligently the welfare of its community; to offer suggestions, but to abhor any tone of superior wisdom; to join in all possible common ventures for community improvement; and to encourage its faculty and staff to serve and contribute as *local citizens* in any beneficial community activity. Faculty members, for example, are doubly concerned with education, as both teachers and parents. There are specialists in a dozen fields who, with an appropriate accommodation in their approach, can help solve community problems. Administrators can serve on boards and committees. The wives of the faculty are a rich resource of talent, if zeal for progress is tempered by political understanding of the attitudes of people not blessed with a college degree. Students can serve in many ways in community programs for young people.

In sum, the liberal university must keep its head in the sky in order to see the world, but it must remember that its feet should be firmly placed on the ground of its local community. Whether that ground is rough or slippery or smooth and solid is the result of patience, understanding, and intelligence on the part of all concerned over many years. There is no magic formula in community relations. Respect and goodwill are likely to be the unsought dividends of being a good neighbor.

2

RELATIONS WITH FOUNDATIONS

The critical means of survival and growth for the private liberal college or university has long been found in the generous support of persons of wealth. Tuition income has become more important as institutions have broken away from the long-depressing influence of conventional tuition rates. But the quality and freedom of a private, liberal university, the steady strengthening of its faculty, the ability to enroll able students regardless of means, as well as the adequacy and beauty of its structures and campus, are in great measure the consequence of the thoughtful generosity of dedicated alumni and friends.

In recent decades, a great system of philanthropic foundations has come to intervene between the generous individual donor
and the private liberal university, especially in those situations
where large funds are involved. There are many practical reasons
for this development, and great good has been done; but the intervention of third parties, with their own prestige, policies, and predilections, into the stream of support has introduced complications
and issues for the university.

The basic problems in the relations of the university and the
foundations are: Which of the two well-meaning agencies should
be *primarily* responsible for the initiation of expensive programs of
instruction, research, or service, and which should sustain the continuing cost of these programs once established? The foundation,
with men of ideas on its board and staff, prides itself on searching
out areas of instruction, scholarship, or service which offer new
and strategic possibilities of contribution to national or global welfare. Usually it prefers to be a temporary catalyst of growth within
the university which accepts its ideas and to avoid long-run involvement as the new area of learning ceases to be novel and
becomes an increasing drain on the university budget.

To revert to the growing-tree analogy used earlier in the discussion of curricular controls, the foundation would like to stimulate the growth of a new branch on some larger limb of the tree
for a while but assume that the roots and trunk will meanwhile
develop the strength and sap to sustain and nourish the new
branch in years to come. The question is: How many and what
kind of new branches can the tree develop by external stimulation
yet maintain its stability, balance, integration, and general health?

In earlier years, there were deficit areas in the curricular structure of many universities, or there were needed services which they
had not come to assume. The wise foundation was concerned with
filling these deficits, and the process helped to round out the
general contribution of the university. As time has passed, the
dynamic university, with its constant pressure for differentiation,
has gone far to fill the deficit areas, even with the expanding needs
of the world. Given the tradition, mission, and general resources of
the particular university, the total program came closer to struc-

tural and functional balance. In filling out reasonably related areas, the university assumed an appropriate responsibility to maintain those areas by every means at its command.

But as time has passed and costs have risen sharply, the attention of university leadership in private institutions has had to be focused, not so much on deficits in its curricular structure, but more and more on deficits in the total budget to pay higher faculty and staff salaries and larger service costs on structures and facilities (including libraries, laboratories, and computers), and to provide financial support and living accommodations for able but penurious students. These are not exciting areas for foundations interested in new ideas. Yet any *private* university, at least, which has sought or accepted a temporary grant for a new curricular or research project, was increasing the probability of a general financial deficit at the same time that it was filling a deficit in its academic program.

The foundation executive, on his part, can readily say that it is up to the administration of a university to keep its financial house in order and that he is not interested in *general* budgets. But he knows as well as anyone else the nature of a university and that academic freedom promotes the development of challenging and expensive ideas on the part of many professors. It is, however, more interesting to be a pioneer and to talk with pioneering people. To talk with treasurers and deans of faculty seeking to meet budgets and competing salary offers is a bread-and-butter bore. Yet the treasurers and deans of faculty are faced with problems affecting the survival and future health of the private, liberal university far more than are those who believe that an institution needs to teach more African languages or to find out how porpoises communicate.

Those concerned with the survival and the balanced growth in quality and coverage of the private, liberal university are not asking too much of the foundation that it remember that in many cases the foundations have taken over the function of the wealthy, individual donor who long contributed to the basic, general support of the private institution. The names of buildings, professorships, scholarship and fellowship endowments, and many other funds serving and supporting basic functions which appear in the catalogue of any older university will show this clearly. While new ideas are good, the old idea of a healthy going concern is even better. The foundation cannot take over a vital flow of wealth without assuming some obligation to fulfill the intent of those farsighted and generous individuals who, in the past, realized that a tree must be strong and vigorous throughout in order to support new branches.

The least that the foundation can be asked to provide, in their interest in new ventures, is the full overhead cost of such ventures. The time is past in most institutions when the complex and costly supporting services now required could be spread over more activities without severe strain. It is now necessary, in avoiding future deficits, to assign the cost of faculty and staff benefits (as well as direct salaries), of space and service requirements, and of all general administrative services in proper proportion to each new venture. The university's accounting must be even more exact and conservative than that in industry, since its income is less susceptible to control. Further, an industrial corporation can merge or go out of business. It does not have hundreds of higher-salaried employees on permanent tenure. The cost of a new idea is the full and continuing cost of its implementation, not just the marginal, direct increment which is immediately visible.

It is the hope of the university administrator that the boards and executives of the larger foundation will fully recognize and understand the anatomy and physiology of the liberal, private university in its mature state and in the political economy which now exists. The continuing private foundation and the permanent private university have much in common. Both contribute a precious ingredient of intellectual free enterprise in an ongoing democratic society. Smaller foundations with more rigidly specified missions might do well, it is believed, to assign their resources, after a reasonable period, to such universities as seem best fitted to carry out their general purposes. The overhead for administration and for the determination of new ventures within the university would be much less than that in most small foundations. Further, the university can move over the years with the changing needs of society and can avoid the problems which so often develop in the legalistic interpretation of the intent of small charitable trusts.

In all that has been said, there is no suggestion that the university has a monopoly on new ideas in the advancement of knowledge or in the development of educational methods. Even the strongest and most dynamic of university departments may become caught in their own momentum. Compared to a foundation, however, a university faculty has a built-in pluralism and a freewheeling initiative well insulated from conformity to any higher command. Even the ablest university administration can become cozy and overcautious, but it deals with teacher-scholars whose tenure and status in their discipline give special weight to their ideas. Further, the rapid intercommunication of ideas among the leaders in a discipline throughout the country assures a compounding of catalytic interaction among leading institutions. The foundations, as external catalysts, have a valuable role to play in adding a further source of pluralistic initiative, with the great advantage that their ideas can be backed by financial support. It is important, however, that, in the competition for the limited funds generally available to advance fundamental scholarship and research, the primary justification for support be the idea in itself and not its place of birth. The university asks two things of the foundation in playing its role: first, that it understand the nature and ongoing needs of the modern university as an integrated, total institution; and, second, that it help perpetuate the great values of academic freedom by a balanced recognition of the great values of academic foresight. The large foundation, if it wants, can encourage a private liberal university to become a livery stable of teacher-scholars of high talent whose connection with the university becomes incidental. For a while, this might produce spectacular results. But the time would come when the liberal, private university, as such, would falter and lose momentum. Perhaps the state would come to its rescue. But gradually and surely something would go out of American higher education—a centuries-old tradition of independence and pluralism.

The foundation can help the liberal university in many specific ways apart from larger new ventures and within the terms already suggested. Without invading the precious sense of responsibility of the faculty member for teaching and for the good order and welfare of his institution in general, it can help him continue to grow through support on leaves for scholarship and in the total program of scholarship and research in which he is already engaged. The strength of a university is, again, its faculty, not today alone, but for years to come, working in a strong university with stimulating colleagues and students. In helping to sustain the quality and vigor of the faculty of a liberal university, the foundation is investing in the university's most critical resource for the benefit of generations to come.

❧ 3 ❧

RELATIONS
WITH
THE
GENERAL
PUBLIC

In its relations with the general public, the liberal university with limited, selective enrollment faces a subtle but persistent paradox in the attitudes of a large segment of the American people. On the one hand, no kind of social system needs a broader flow of potential leaders than a free society dependent upon pluralistic initiative to sustain its progress. Such a flow seems to be taken for granted. Yet the members of a prosperous democratic society tend to become increasingly egalitarian in their attitudes and to question any institution or activity which suggests the correlative condition that there are differences in the leadership potentialities of people.

While *leadership* is accepted as a necessary ingredient in effective organized activity, the potential *leader*, or any agency which is concerned with his development, is slightly suspect. American leaders and the institutions which seek to produce them must constantly "prove" that they are "democratic," especially if by exceptional effort they have attained a position which suggests "privilege."

The justification for the existence of an expensive, interactive kind of higher education here termed "liberal education" is that it is an effective and socially beneficial means of enhancing the flow of leaders for the society it serves. Because it is relatively expensive and geared to the education of persons of higher-than-average talent, it must limit its rate of growth and must be selective in its admissions. These factors combine to suggest that it serves a "privileged" segment of its society, no matter how hard it strives to make individual potential rather than personal financial resources the criterion for admission.

The attitude of the general public which intimates that the liberal university, and especially the older, private liberal university, is in some sense a carry-over of a tradition of "privilege" into a classless, egalitarian society is influenced by many factors, real and assumed. Among these are: the image of the American liberal university as a transplanted Oxford or Cambridge with their persistent overtones of status in a stratified society; the great emphasis upon distinguished architecture, and upon beautiful surroundings on many campuses; the manifestations of institutional pride and loyalty by students and alumni which come to have social overtones; and the ambitions of parents to enroll their children in a "prestige" institution to assure them a status in life through association and not by merit alone. Such factors, apart from the truly educational functions of the older liberal university, make it the object of a mixture of attitudes reflecting both the increasing egalitarianism of a classless society and yet the persistent desire of ambitious individuals to advance their status within that society.

The effects of this inherent paradox upon the public relations of the liberal university are complex. With a high degree of visibility and the American suspicion of "privilege," any untoward event on a university campus receives far wider attention than it may deserve. Long before the disturbances at Berkeley or on Morningside Heights, a riot, a questionable speaker, a fraternity exposé, or a one-sided account of social life on campus was certain to stimulate journalists and commentators to exploit the questioning attitude and the special curiosity of the general public concerning a "privileged" sector of American life.

A story is told of President McCosh reprimanding the students at Princeton in the 1870's after a riotous evening. At chapel the next morning, the beloved old Scotsman closed with the exhortation: "Boys, boys, don't carry on that way! Whenever you do, the next day it's in the New York papers and the day after that it's in the Philadelphia papers!" Except for the speeding up of communications, there has been little change in the century since then in the readiness of city editors to give space to the unseemly behavior of college students.

Recent disturbances on a number of university campuses, here and abroad, have made the university a focus of greater public attention than at any time in recent memory. However, history is replete with student rebellions since medieval times. The reasons for student unrest at this time have already been discussed. Despite the serious losses in time, energy, and immediate contribution which the recent disturbances have caused, they have brought an age-old type of institution to the attention of millions of people who have, perhaps, taken them too much for granted. Universities, as in centuries past, will learn much from their troubles. It is hoped that the public will also learn something about a type of institution which gives vitality to a society.

It is probably true that the liberal university will always be subject to more public attention than it would prefer with respect to the less significant aspects of its way of life. It is probably too much to expect the *general* newspaper press, the radio commentator, or commercial television to present much material on the scholarly contributions, scientific discoveries, or the normal educational operations which are in the mainstream of the university's activities. Except for sports and more spectacular scientific developments, the *general* public is not much interested.

The coverage of news concerning the intellectual aspects of university and college activity has, however, increased in recent years in several of the outstanding newspapers of the country with sufficient staff to have specialists in science, art, literature, and education itself. The news weeklies have broadened their coverage of university developments in their special sections assigned to education, science, medicine, and the arts. The "quality" monthly magazines with a readership heavily composed of college graduates have paid increasing attention to higher education. But it is still true that controversy and novelty, although often peripheral, gain far more attention than the educational and scholarly activities which are the mainstream of university life. Since the journalist or editor cannot depart too far from the indicated interest of his readers, the educator must weigh his effectiveness in helping to make university activities interesting.

The great majority of university professors are not prone to demonstrate their wares in ways which interest the general reader. The work of many is in fields too abstruse to make understandable in ordinary English. There are, however, a few professors who come to have a sense of mission in communicating significant findings to the public. A few highly articulate professors become public figures and are quoted on any subject which they may care to discuss. Their standing in their particular discipline is likely to decline as their public visibility rises. By far the largest number of able scholars and scientists are, however, more concerned with advancing their specialized endeavors and with their standing with their academic peers. Experience has shown that a cautious statement concerning preliminary findings has little news appeal. To enlarge on the importance of one's contribution to knowledge may help in university public relations, but not in a professor's relations with his colleagues throughout the country.

It is also difficult to make innovation in educational policies and methods of interest to the general public without the exaggeration of novelty. Few policies or methods in education are new to the world even though they are new to a particular institution. Further, it takes some years to test out a new approach in a process as dependent upon response as higher education. Many experiments which were announced with much enthusiasm in past years have quietly disappeared. It is usually wise to delay public announcement of new ventures in education until they have ceased to be news.

To avoid dependence upon the editorial judgement of the public press, many universities have developed publications of their own to convey their image to the general public. These go beyond the usual series of catalogues and announcements intended for students and the alumni magazines of interest to graduates. Some are mailing pieces describing interesting teaching and research programs. Others take on the quality of distinguished quarterlies with articles written by authors in some way associated with the university. To attract a broader spectrum of readers, the subjects covered include a wide range of intellectual, political, and scientific developments, as well as those in higher education. Carefully edited and well designed, such magazines are an expensive investment in transmitting an institutional image. Focused on a readership most likely to understand the role of the liberal university, they are probably a sound investment at a time when such understanding is a precious resource.

A steady builder of understanding of the nature of a liberal university as a community of scholars is a well-directed university press. It is true, however, that the carry-over to the general public is secondary to the impression made on the world of fellow scholars and intellectuals. Few books from university presses appear on the racks of drugstores, even in paperback editions, nor are learned journals found on newsstands.

The freedom of the faculty to avoid the task of giving public visibility to the university's mission is not available to the president. In season and out, regardless of the inches of print resulting, the president of a liberal university must interpret its mission to the world. The presidency of a distinguished institution is still a position of respect among millions of people who know little of what goes on in the institution. It is not difficult for the president to acquire appointments representing the public on boards and commissions. It is harder for him to get his message across when he is discussing his main business, the assurance of good health and progress in higher education. Probably the most immediate effect in public relations is gained when the president declares the position of the university in some situation he would prefer to avoid.

The most effective channel of public relations available to the liberal university in the rough seas ahead is found in its alumni as the products of its educational efforts. By assuming positions of leadership in hundreds of communities, large and small, the graduates of an institution whose mission is to develop leaders serve as visible examples of what liberal education can contribute. The desire of the alumnus to encourage able young persons to attend his alma mater or his loyalty to it in sports may be taken by others as a forgivable display of sentiment, but when, time after time, it is the graduate of a liberal university who takes on the job of improving the standards of a community in government, education, welfare, cultural expression, or urban development, the corelation between education and leadership becomes a bit clearer.

In a democracy faced by a multitude of problems in a time of change and stress, the liberal university can, it is hoped, rely upon its alumni more than ever before to demonstrate its contribution. The more the world changes, the more some persistent elements are clear. Leadership is always at a premium and will be recognized. Institutions which seek to enhance the qualities of leadership will do well to focus their efforts upon that task and let the results be their main source of public approval.

A promising indication that the liberal university can rely upon its alumni to demonstrate its contribution before the public is the increasing recognition by the industrial and financial corporations of America that a liberal education is a valuable preparation for the toughest jobs in corporate leadership—at the top. The American corporation is now a perpetual institution dependent upon imaginative insight and sensitive understanding to prosper in a world of complex and rapidly changing relations with governments, communities, organized labor, supervisory and technical staffs, consumers, and other corporations and institutions. While the corporation can hire a multitude of specialists, it must develop a leadership which resolves these into a viable human organization with a personality of its own.

To help in this challenging task, an education aimed at enhancing the understanding of human response, the powers of analysis, judgment, and communication, a sense of history, and intellectual and moral integrity is indeed vocational in the highest sense. The corporation, with its increasing influence upon American life, along with government, needs the product of the liberal university more than ever before. The *private* liberal university, to assure its freedom of initiative, needs, in turn, the help of the *private* corporation which employs its graduates in positions of leadership and depends upon its contributions to knowledge in crossing new frontiers. The business of a liberal university is the advancement of knowledge and the education of young persons for leadership. This is a business which the American corporation, as a key segment of the American "public," has come to understand without the aid of press releases or radio broadcasts. The best media in the public relations of a liberal university are, indeed, the leaders it has helped to develop, not only for industry, but for all the challenging vocations in a democratic society.

FACULTY
RECOMMENDATION
FORMS
USED AT
PRINCETON
UNIVERSITY

A. For recommending reappointments, promotions, and salary changes.

FORM Z. For recommendations of reappointments, promotions, or changes in salary concerned with ranks above that of instructor and for the reappointment of an instructor to a fourth or fifth year of service. Please typewrite, if possible.

PRINCETON UNIVERSITY

To the Dean of the Faculty
For Transmission to the President:

Date ....

The Department of ....

recommends the { reappointment / promotion / Change in salary } of ....

Recommended rank .... *Recommended salary $................................

Present rank ...., *Present salary $...

for a term of .... year......., from .... to ....

* If salary is stated on other than an academic year basis, please indicate in respect to both current and recommended salary. If salary is to be charged in part or in whole to other than general departmental account, please indicate the amounts and accounts to be charged.

This recommendation, and the appraisal given on the following pages, were approved

{ by unanimous vote / by majority vote } at a meeting of. { the professors / the associate professors / the assistant professors } of the Department

on ....

....
Chairman of Department

DO NOT WRITE BELOW THIS LINE

1. Received by Dean of the Faculty:

2. Action by Advisory Committee:

3. Recommendation of President to Curriculum Committee of the Trustees:

4. Action by the Board of Trustees:

(OVER)

APPENDIX

This recommendation has been made on the basis of the following appraisal of his qualifications:

AS A TEACHER:

1. General effectiveness as a teacher

2. Detailed appraisal:

   (a) As teacher of graduate students

   (b) As teacher of upperclassmen

   (c) As teacher of underclassmen

   (d) As lecturer

   (e) As preceptor

   (f) As supervisor of departmental students

   (g) As class-room instructor

   (h) As laboratory supervisor

AS A SCHOLAR:

1. General standing as a scholar. Indicate fields of special competence.

2. List his more significant publications, with dates, and, in the case of periodicals, with full volume and page reference. Which of these publications are primarily addressed to specialists? Which to a wider audience of intelligent readers? Which of them are school or college text books? (If necessary, attach a separate sheet for this list.)

3. What has been the verdict of other scholars on any of these writings? Name the scholars, briefly summarize their opinions, and indicate where the opinions have been expressed.

(OVER)

4. In what ways other than teaching and writing has his scholarship been shown?

5. What promise does he give of further growth and productivity as a scholar?

AS A FACULTY-MEMBER:

1. In what ways other than as teacher and writer has he made effective contributions to the work of his department or of the university?

For the Department of ....

....
Chairman of Department

B. For recommending new professorial appointments.

FORM W. For recommendations of new appointments above the grade of instructor. Please typewrite, if possible.

PRINCETON UNIVERSITY

TO THE DEAN OF THE FACULTY
FOR TRANSMISSION TO THE PRESIDENT:

Date..

The Department of ....

recommends the appointment of ....

Recommended rank .... * Recommended salary $..

for a term of .... year .... from .... to ....

* If salary is stated on other than an academic year basis, please indicate. If salary is to be charged in part or in whole to other than general departmental account, please indicate both amounts and accounts to be charged.

This recommendation, and the appraisal given on the following pages, were approved

$\left\{ \begin{array}{l} \text{by unanimous vote} \\ \text{by majority vote} \end{array} \right\}$ at a meeting of $\left\{ \begin{array}{l} \text{the professors} \\ \text{the associate professors} \\ \text{the assistant professors} \end{array} \right.$ of the Department

on ....

....
Chairman

Note: Has candidate been advised of arrangements covering annuities and group insurance?

DO NOT WRITE BELOW THIS LINE

1. Received by Dean of the Faculty:

2. Action by Advisory Committee:

3. Recommendation of President to Curriculum Committee of the Trustees:

4. Action by the Board of Trustees:

(OVER)

Birthday .... Married .... Living children ....

Place of birth .... Citizenship ....

Educational record (institutions attended, dates, degrees)

Record of previous teaching appointments (institutions, dates, ranks, subjects)

Record of other experience (war service, government service, industrial or professional experience, dates)

Principal publications with dates, publishers, page references, etc. (Use separate sheet if more convenient.)

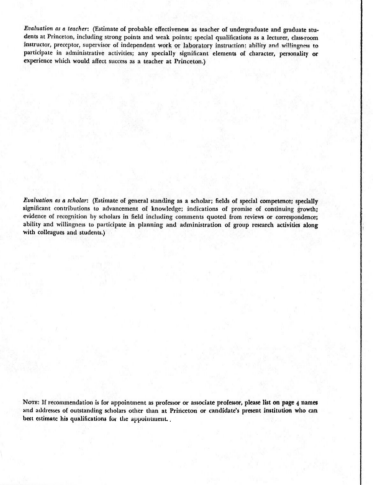

Evaluation as a teacher: (Estimate of probable effectiveness as teacher of undergraduate and graduate students at Princeton, including strong points and weak points; special qualifications as a lecturer, class-room instructor, preceptor, supervisor of independent work or laboratory instruction: ability and willingness to participate in administrative activities; any specially significant elements of character, personality or experience which would affect success as a teacher at Princeton.)

Evaluation as a scholar: (Estimate of general standing as a scholar; fields of special competence; specially significant contributions to advancement of knowledge; indications of promise of continuing growth; evidence of recognition by scholars in field including comments quoted from reviews or correspondence; ability and willingness to participate in planning and administration of group research activities along with colleagues and students.)

NOTE: If recommendation is for appointment as professor or associate professor, please list on page 4 names and addresses of outstanding scholars other than at Princeton or candidate's present institution who can best estimate his qualifications for the appointment. .

INDEX

INDEX

This book was set in Electra by Vail-Ballou Press, Inc., and printed on permanent paper and bound by Vail-Ballou Press, Inc. The designer was J. E. O'Connor. The editors were Steven Melmeck and Helen Greenberg. Peter D. Guilmette supervised the production.